52 Perfect Day Trips

for Fit Adults
in the Greater Washington Area

52 Perfect Day Trips

for Fit Adults
in the Greater Washington Area

by

Beth and David Sansbury

ISBN 978-1-105-51744-0

How This Tour Book is Different

Have you ever bought a tour book only to find that the authors were iron men and women—60-mile bike trips and 25-mile hikes? Well, this book is for the fit but not fanatic adult. It also aims to please those who want to exercise not only brawn but brains. Almost all of the trips devote half of the day to hiking, biking, or kayaking in beautiful surroundings while the other half is devoted to learning—historic houses and towns, museums, and the like. This book is not for tourists from out of town who want to see the White House or the usual museums on the Mall. It is rather for area residents who want to discover something new and exciting in their own backyards. Each trip is no more than one and a half hours outside the Capital Beltway (I-495). The whole day is planned for you, even with a recommended lunch spot. All you need do is set aside the day.

About the Authors

Beth and David Sansbury have lived their whole adult lives in the Washington, DC area and currently live in Great Falls, Virginia. Both are CIA annuitants; he is a psychologist and she is an economist. In addition to biking, kayaking, and hiking, they are also avid pickleball players and enjoy cross-country skiing. They have participated in these activities at home and around the world. They have biked along the Loire, Danube, and Elbe and hiked in Taiwan and Bhutan. The idea for this book came from their love of an active lifestyle and their interest in cultural pursuits and their realization that a day trip could combine the best of both worlds.

Preface

This is the second and completely revised edition of our very popular tour book that was first researched and written more than ten years ago when we semi-retired. We thought how nice it would be to finally have a chance to visit local places and do things for which we had never found time. It was sold in local bookstores, by the National Park Service, and on Amazon. It remained timely until COVID hit, and many chosen spots went out of business and/or schedules were changed drastically.

Despite the need to make major revisions, our goals remain the same: plan a full day of activities, including a lunch spot, choose trips that are inexpensive (many are free), and limit the travel time to less than one and a half hours outside the Capital Beltway. The emphasis is, indeed, outside the Beltway, and only three trips are included that are in Washington DC, chosen because they are off the beaten track and are in sylvan settings.

A few notes about using this guide:

- The Beltway is used as our starting point, and directions are given from there. These directions are minimal in recognition of the fact that virtually everyone now uses travel apps such as Waze.

- Because everyone does not own a kayak or canoe, we have chosen mostly water trips that have rentals onsite. Those that don't include access to interesting trails for walking or hiking. Trip 49 is the only exception, requiring you to bring your own boat.

- This is not a restaurant guide. If we found a lunch spot befitting the occasion—casual if it followed biking or hiking—and if it had tasty food, we included it. Other choices may be equally good

- If a Visitor Center is available, please drop by for the free maps and guides. These give you additional information, and, more importantly, the local personnel can tell you of any dangers to avoid and seasonal sights to see.

- Hardly anyone travels today without doing some online research. Take advantage of the web sites listed in our information boxes.

- We have made every effort to make this guide as accurate as possible, but many things can change over time. Please help us keep it up to date and let us know how you think it can be improved. E-mail us at: mesansbury@yahoo.com.

CONTENTS BY AREA

KEY
(B)=Biking *(H)*=Hiking *(W)*=Walking
(K)=Kayaking/Canoeing

MARYLAND

WASHINGTON, DC

VIRGINIA

WEST VIRGINIA

CONTENTS BY TYPE OF ACTIVITY

KEY
(M)=Maryland *(DC)*=Washington DC
(V)=Virginia *(WVa)*=West Virginia

BIKING

HIKING

KAYAKING/CANOEING

WALKING (all day walking but not hiking trips)

Trip 1 – An Arty Day: The Walters Art Museum and The Baltimore Museum of Art

WHY: See collections that span the globe and, although smaller than the museums on the Mall, they are no less significant.

WHERE: Both museums are in the same general area of north Baltimore—off Charles Street—but not within walking distance of each other. For the Walters, a parking lot is located across the street at Centre and Cathedral Streets. Metered parking is in front of the BMA.

HOW LONG: In about four hours you can do the highlights of the collections, or you can do specialties or temporary exhibits in both places. The Walters has a self-guided tour called "Our Collection in One Hour" starting in the Walters Centre Street Building.

LUNCH BREAK: We recommend that you go to the Walters first, have a quick lunch, and then head up to the BMA. You can either eat at the Walters' newly renovated café on the first level or take a short walk to the **Trinacria Café**, at 111 W. Center St. and eat at a wonderful Italian market serving daily specials.

HIGHLIGHTS: **The Walters Art Museum** collection was amassed substantially by two men, William and Henry Walters, and eventually bequeathed to the City of Baltimore. The collection ranges from pre- dynastic Egypt to twentieth century Europe and counts among its treasures Greek sculpture and Roman sarcophagi; medieval ivories; Old Master paintings; and Art Deco jewelry. It also has a particularly rich collection of art from India, Nepal and Tibet. Its temporary exhibits change frequently.

The internationally renowned Cone Collection of modern

art is the crown jewel of **The Baltimore Museum of Art**. In the early 20th Century, Baltimore sisters Claribel and Etta Cone made frequent visits to Paris, where they visited the studios of Henri Matisse and Pablo Picasso, which spurred their life-long obsession with collecting art. They acquired some 3,000 objects—including the largest holdings of Henri Matisse in the world, which are now housed in a special wing of the museum. The BMA also exhibits European Masters of the fifteenth through nineteenth centuries, a rich African collection, and an amazing photo collection that includes cutting edge photographers such as Steichen and Man Ray. The atrium on the main floor is papered in Roman mosaics lifted from Antioch, Syria. Outside, the beautiful sculpture gardens are open year-round except in inclement weather.

The BMA is also the site of "Gertrude's Chesapeake Kitchen", featuring farm-fresh food that preserves Chesapeake culinary traditions. The dining room overlooks the sculpture garden featuring works by Calder, Noguchi, and Rodin.

Since October 2006, both the Baltimore Museum of Art and the Walters Art Museum offer free general admission year-round as a result of grants given by Baltimore City, Baltimore County, and several foundations.

MORE INFORMATION

The Walters Art Museum
thewalters.org
600 N. Charles St., Baltimore
410-547-9000
Open Wednesday-Sunday, 10am-5pm
Thursday, 1-8pm
Entrance free

Baltimore Museum of Art
artbma.org
10 Art Museum Drive, Baltimore
443-573-1700
Open Wednesday-Sunday, 10am-5pm
Thursday, 10am-8pm
Entrance free
Search and view thousands of objects from the
collection on its website.

Trip 2 – Scientific-Visionary Day in South Baltimore

WHY: Quirky little South Baltimore is home to two fascinating museums—the Maryland Science Center and the American Visionary Art Museum, both of which have great views of the harbor. A bonus is a charming neighborhood market that provides some local color and seafood for lunch.

WHERE: Go to the Maryland Science Museum first, eat lunch at the Cross Street Market, and then visit the Visionary Art Museum, a few blocks down the street in front of Federal Hill.

HOW LONG: The drive to Baltimore after rush hour from the Capital Beltway takes about an hour. A couple of hours in each museum will allow you to see the main exhibits. Allow an extra 45 minutes in the Maryland Science Center if you want to catch an IMAX film or a planetarium show.

LUNCH BREAK: From the Maryland Science Museum, go south on Light Street for seven blocks until you come to the **Cross Street Market**, there since 1845 and completely renovated in 2019. The 22 independently owned eateries range from crabs to vegan organics. Then get back on Light Street and turn right on Key Highway to go to the second museum.

HIGHLIGHTS: The **Maryland Science Center** is a magnet for local school kids, but it is equally appealing to adults. Its three floors pack in quality exhibits on dinosaurs, Mother Earth, the body, and space, among others. Many of them are hands-on. Newton's Alley is real "physical science" and allows you to play a string-less harp, touch a cloud, see sound, and convert your energy to electricity. The center also has a five-story IMAX theater and the Davis Planetarium, which uses special effects to explore the cosmos.

The **American Visionary Art Museum** is a treasure house of self-taught and intuitive artistry and must be seen to be believed, as they say. These pieces of art were created by farmers, housewives, mechanics, retirees, the disabled, the homeless, and even the occasional neurosurgeon. They include carved roots and graphite pencils, embroidered rags, toothpick and matchstick edifices, birds-eye photographs of wheat field designs, and a room in praise of OCD (obsessive-compulsive disorder) as an inspiration for art. An adjacent large barn of a building houses Baltimore's own row house-painted window screen art, a large number of whirligigs that can be set in motion by the visitor, and a car decorated with blue bottles and assorted junk. Almost as interesting as the art are the labels detailing the life stories of the artists and what fired their creative drive.

Their permanent collection is self-described as "one small speck in a Bling universe where art reflects life, both literally and figuratively. Adorning one's world—transforming it into a place that defies convention, surprising and delighting, providing hope and wonder—is what the Bling Universe is all about."

MORE INFORMATION

Maryland Science Center

www.mdsci.org
601 Light Street, Baltimore
410-685-5225
Open Tuesday-Friday, 10am-4pm
    Saturday and Sunday, 10am-5pm
Entrance fee $26.95/adult, $25.95/senior

American Visionary Art Museum

www.avam.org
800 Key Highway (at Covington), Baltimore
410-244-1900
Open Tuesday-Sunday, 10am-6pm
Entrance fee $15.95/adult, $13.95/senior

Cross Street Market

crossstmarket.com
1065 S. Charles Street

Trip 3 – Boats and Trains in Baltimore

WHY: Go just south of Baltimore Harbor to find good flat-water kayaking launched from the site of a fort built during the Spanish-American War. Go just north of the Harbor to tour the phenomenal B&O Railroad Museum that celebrates America's first railroad.

WHERE: Your kayaking destination is Fort Smallwood Park, an Anne Arundel County Park that was transferred from Baltimore City in 2009. For those who didn't bring their kayaks, there are good walking trails and remnants of the fort to explore. After working up an appetite, your next destination is Nick's Fish House and then a short drive into the city to the B&O Railroad Museum.

HOW LONG: The drive from the Capital Beltway to the put-in point at Fort Smallwood is about 40 minutes. We spent one and a half hours paddling. The drive to Nick's from the wharf is about 30 minutes and then to the B&O Railroad Museum just 10 minutes. The Museum can easily occupy you for a couple of hours.

LUNCH BREAK: **Nick's Fish House** (2600 Insulator Drive) offers "casual waterfront dining," which says it all. Crabs—delectably fat—-and other seafood are the specialty.

HIGHLIGHTS: Putting your boat in at **Fort Smallwood** (look for signs to the Boat Ramp) allows you two choices—staying in the little inlet called "Rock Creek" lined with modest houses and enjoying the bird life that accompanies your paddling or heading for open water to look at the famous white rocks in the Bay, a geologic landmark. This also provides a view of the huge Sparrows point steel plant, formerly owned by Bethlehem Steel.

Fort Smallwood from 1896 to 1928 was a coastal fort, a part of harbor defenses during the Spanish-American War. It was named for Revolutionary War Maj. Gen. Smallwood (1732-1792), commander of the "Maryland Line" regiment in the Continental Army who later became the fourth governor of Maryland. A Baltimore city park from 1928 to 2006, it was an extremely popular weekend picnicking, swimming and fishing site, later eclipsed by ocean resorts after the construction of the Chesapeake Bay Bridge in 1952.

The **Baltimore and Ohio Railroad Museum** is a major attraction, containing the oldest and most comprehensive American railroad collection in the country. It is the birthplace of American railroading because it was here within the Museum's 40-acre campus that the first commercial long-distance track was laid and the first passenger station built. Fittingly, it is a National Historic Landmark and an affiliate of the Smithsonian. The museum site is huge with many things to see. There is an architecturally stunning roundhouse— packed with trains of all kinds and interesting well-explained exhibits—and two model railroads, one outside and another in a train car. The Mile One Express Train takes visitors on a 20-minute round trip ride along the first mile of laid track. On the weekends, the train ride can be combined with a stop at the state-of-the-art Restoration Shop. Choo-Choo Blueville, for younger children, is a beautifully landscaped fictional town that has 12 miniature buildings and a three-minute kiddie train ride.

MORE INFORMATION

Fort Smallwood Park
en.wikipedia.org/wiki/Fort_Smallwood_Park

B&O Railroad Museum
www.borail.org
901 West Pratt Street, Baltimore
410-752-2490
Open Monday-Sunday, 10am-4pm
Mile One Express runs from April-December on
Thursday and Friday at 11:30am, Saturday at
11:30am and 2pm, and Sunday at 1pm. Check
website for other times of year
Entrance fee $18/adult, $16/senior
Train ride $3/adult

Fort Smallwood

Trip 4 – House and Garden North of Baltimore

WHY: Ladew Topiary Gardens are known around the world for their more than 100 topiaries and flower gardens on their 22-acre property. Not far away, Hampton House, when it was finished in 1790, was the largest house in the US and remains a showplace today.

WHERE: Both sites are north of Baltimore (Monkton and Towson) in Baltimore County, enabling you to use both the Capital Beltway and the Baltimore Beltway to get there.

HOW LONG: The drive to Ladew, the furthest point, is about one and one-half hours from the Washington Beltway. Spend the morning there, have lunch at their café and then head for Hampton House, about a half-hour away. You will easily have two hours to explore each site.

LUNCH BREAK: The **Ladew Café** offers a delicious but limited menu featuring artisan sandwiches, salads, and sweets dished up by Harford County's popular "Eats and Sweets".

HIGHLIGHTS: **Ladew Topiary Gardens** is the vision of Harvey S. Ladew (1887-1976), a self-taught gardener who became fascinated in the 1920s with the art of English topiary—the training and trimming of ornamental shrubs into sculptural shapes. His Hunt Scene is internationally known—a horse jumping a hurdle after hounds and a fox. He was one of the first Americans to create thematic "garden rooms" devoted to a single color, plant, or theme.

The historic Manor House, equestrian-inspired, offers 30-minute docent-guided tours all week. There is also a mile-long nature walk and a native Butterfly House open from early July through early October that is included in the price of admission.

Hampton House, now administered as a National Park Service Historic Site, was built by American sea Captain Charles Ridgely. The Ridgely property once equaled half the area of present-day Baltimore and was the source of iron ore production and valuable agricultural crops. The Georgian mansion was built in 1790 to impress, and it still does today. The home was lived in by Ridgely heirs until 1948, and the lavish furnishings reflect the expensive tastes of successive owners.

The second master of the estate was known for his fine thoroughbred horses, marking the beginning of Maryland's reputation as the center of American racing. The grounds include an elaborate icehouse, an orangery, and a formal parterre garden. Tours and occasional lectures focus on the history of the property and the people who lived there, including the enslaved and European indentured servants.

MORE INFORMATION

Ladew Topiary Gardens
> www.ladewgardens.com
> 3535 Jarrettsville Pike, Monkton
> 410-557-9466
> Gardens open daily, closed Wednesdays
> April 1-October 31, 9am-4pm
> Guided manor house tours: weekdays 11am, noon,
> 1pm, 2 pm, weekends 11am-3:30 every half hour
> Entrance fee to house and gardens $17/adult,
> $12/senior

Hampton National Historic Site
> www.nps.gov/hamp
> 535 Hampton Lane, Towson
> 410-823-1309
> Visitor center open Thursday-Sunday, 9am-4pm
> Grounds open daily, 8:30-5pm except holidays
> Mansion tours are 45-60 minutes; visitors must
> get tickets on day of tour; tours are free but
> fill up fast. Consult website.

Trip 5 – Biking Through Farm Country in Carroll County

WHY: Carroll County is one of Maryland's loveliest rural counties, and Westminster, the county seat, is home to a fascinating farm museum that sponsors a full schedule of special events, including the Maryland Wine Festival in September. It is also home to McDaniel College, formerly Western Maryland College, founded in 1867, the first coeducational college south of the Mason-Dixon Line.

WHERE: From the Capital Beltway, the best route is to take I-270 north toward Frederick and exit on SR355 at Germantown toward Mt. Airy. Follow the signs to Westminster along Ridge Road (SR27). Turn right before Westminster at Kate Wagner Road and follow the signs to the Carroll County Farm Museum, where you can park while you take your 15-mile circular bike tour.

HOW LONG: The drive to Westminster takes at most one and a half hours, and the bike ride takes another two. Add an hour for a leisurely tour of the Farm Museum. See optional extension at end.

LUNCH BREAK: Westminster, being a college town, has many interesting cafes. While on our bike tour, we lunched at **Moll's Cafe** (199 E. Main Street) on the southeast side of town, a local mom-and-pop that has excellent shrimp salad sandwiches, turkey clubs and waffles.

HIGHLIGHTS: The Bike Ride around Westminster starts at the Farm Museum. Bike south on Gist Road, left on Smith Ave., and right on SR32. After crossing SR97, you turn left onto Deer Park Road, where you leave the traffic behind and start enjoying the sweet smells of the green countryside. At the Deer Park turnoff is an old Methodist Church converted to "The Maryland Store." A new church was built across the road, leaving its huge cemetery behind The Maryland Store. The store has Maryland souvenirs of all kinds—from a full complement of Old Bay seasonings to "crabby" ties and socks. In two miles, turn left on Green Mill Road and turn left again onto Old Westminster Pike. Don't worry about traffic because it's all on the Interstate between Baltimore and Frederick. Ride into Westminster, rich in history and tradition, where Civil War troops from both sides trekked and camped on their fateful march to Gettysburg. Main Street has three nineteenth century buildings under the auspices of the Historical Society of Carroll County (at 210 E. Main St.) where you will find an exhibition gallery and displays of historic toys and dolls (closed on Mondays). Have lunch and then pedal up to McDaniel College, which has the best views of the surrounding countryside.

Ride back to the center of the town and turn right at Center Street to reach the 140-acre **Carroll County Farm Museum**. You'll have a glimpse into the workings of a nineteenth century farm and its priceless old farm machinery. There are demonstrations (such as quilting and blacksmithing) on the weekends, but you can see the tools of their craft in their workshops during the week; some workshops have audio tours. Mossy brick walkways lead visitors through gardens of yesteryear—rows of spicy herbs and old-fashioned roses. The farm offers its grounds for traditional arts classes like weaving and spinning. On your way out of town on SR32, enjoy some homemade ice cream at **Hoffman's** (934 Washington Road), in business since 1947—delicious coconut chocolate chip.

If you are interested in a side trip (just 15 minutes from Hoffman's) that explores the roots of early Methodism, visit the **Strawbridge Shrine** in New Windsor. Robert Strawbridge was the first Methodist preacher in America. He was born in Ireland, became converted to Methodism in 1756, and two years later emigrated with his wife to America. For unknown reasons, they chose to settle in New Windsor where he immediately opened his house for worship. John Evans, a local farmer who often helped with chores when Strawbridge was away preaching, became the first recorded Methodist convert. The site features Strawbridge's original house, the Evans House (moved from its original location), the Log Meeting House, a recreation of the first Methodist house of worship in the New World, the Poulson family cemetery, and a Visitor Center.

MORE INFORMATION

Carroll County Farm Museum
> www.carrollcountyfarmmuseum.org
> 500 S. Center Drive, Westminster
> 410-386-3880
> Open Monday-Friday, 9am-4pm
>> Saturday and Sunday, 12pm-4pm (check for
>> winter hours)
> Entrance fee $5/adult, $4/senior

Race Pace Bicycles (for rental)
> 1 Railroad Avenue, Westminster
> 410-876-3001

Strawbridge Shrine
> www.strawbridgeshrine.org
> 2650 Strawbridge Lane, New Windsor
> 443-289-0191
> Open April-October, Friday-Saturday, 10am-4pm,
>> Sunday, 1-4pm
> Call or e-mail to arrange a tour
> Free admission, but donations gratefully accepted

Trip 6 – Biking through the Covered Bridges of Frederick County and a Saintly Detour

WHY: This bike ride around Thurmont goes through two of the three remaining covered bridges in Frederick County—so quaint you think a horse and buggy will emerge any minute. A short ride up US15 is the Grotto of Our Lady of Lourdes and the magnificent Basilica dedicated to Elizabeth Ann Seton, the first native-born citizen of the United States to be canonized (in 1975).

WHERE: After taking I-270 to Frederick and turning north on US15 to Thurmont, take SR77 (Rocky Ridge Road) through Thurmont. Outside town, turn right on Old Frederick Road and you will soon drive through the first covered bridge. Park in Loys Station Park, just past the Bridge. Take the bike ride detailed in the following information box, stopping midway in Thurmont for lunch. After the ride, retrace your steps to US15 and turn north toward Emmittsburg. The Grotto of Lourdes is on the left side of US15, and the National Shrine is on the right side of US15 (Business).

HOW LONG: The drive from the Beltway to the first covered bridge takes no more than an hour. The bike ride of some 17 miles takes about two hours, not counting the lunch stop. Emmittsburg is only 10 minutes from Thurmont. You can spend a couple of hours there at the Grotto and the Seton Shrine with its Visitors Center and Museum.

LUNCH BREAK: **Thurmont Kountry Kitchen Restaurant** (17 Water Street) is about as down home as you can get. It has great food (prize winning broasted chicken) and yummy soft ice treats as well as homemade candy (root beer hard candy went home with us).

HIGHLIGHTS: **The Covered Bridges of Frederick County** were built in the 1850s, part of a move away from stone after the invention of the timber truss. Frederick County has three of the eight bridges still intact in Maryland. All three are still in use.

Loy's Station Covered Bridge, near the car park, has a span of 80 feet and crosses clear and shallow Owens Creek. The bridge on Legore Bridge Road, although not covered, is interesting for its high span above the Monocacy and its well-crafted stone facing. The second covered bridge is the little Roddy Road Bridge, which the Maryland Ghosts and Spirits Association says is haunted by the spirits of Civil War Soldiers killed nearby.

The Grotto of Our Lady of Lourdes is one of the oldest replicas of the revered French shrine and is a popular site for prayer and contemplation in a natural mountain setting. **The National Shrine of Saint Elizabeth Ann Seton** honors the founder of the Sisters of Charity of Saint Joseph. She took an unusual path to sainthood. Born in New York, she married a wealthy businessman, had five children, and was a Protestant. She accompanied her husband to Italy for his health, but he died and she became attracted to Catholicism there. Later, back in the States, she took the vows of a nun and founded the Sisters of Charity as well as Saint Joseph's Free School and Academy. The grounds of the former school have a visitors' center and museum, which was her first permanent home. Also, there are the original Saint Joseph House, the relics of the Saint, and the large ornate Basilica declared by Pope John Paul II to be a "minor basilica."

Directions for Bike Ride: Start at Loys Station Park. Ride away from the bridge on old Frederick Road, turning left on New Cut Road. Turn left on Longs Mill Road and then right on Legore Bridge Road. After admiring the bridge, turn around and get back on Longs Mill Road. Turn right on Creagerstown Road (SR550) and stay on SR550, which becomes E. Main Street. Turn left on Water Street for lunch and then get back on Main Street, turning left on Apples Church Road. This becomes Roddy Road, which goes through the second covered bridge. Retrace your steps into town, turning left on E. Main Street and then turning left on Rocky Ridge Road (SR77). Turn right on Old Frederick Road, and you are back at the car park where you started.

MORE INFORMATION

The National Shrine of Saint Elizabeth Ann Seton
setonshrine.org
333 South Seton Avenue, Emmitsburg
301-447-6606
Basilica: Monday-Sunday, 10am-5pm
Wednesday, 10am-7:30pm
Museum: Monday-Saturday, 10am-5pm
Sunday, 12-5pm
Tours offered multiple times each day (see website)

Grotto of our Lady of Lourdes
msgrotto.org
16330 Grotto Road, Emmitsburg (on the campus
of Mount St. Mary's University)
301-447-5318
Open daily, 9am-4:30pm

Trip 7 – Hiking Catoctin Mountain and Viewing Art in nearby Hagerstown

WHY: See the magnificent recovery of a mountain despoiled in the nineteenth century by logging and iron smelting. FDR was so impressed that he made it his retreat and called it Shangri-La, which President Eisenhower later dubbed Camp David. Hagerstown is home to a notable fine arts museum founded and funded by American impressionist William Henry Singer, Jr.

WHERE: From the Capital Beltway, take I-270 north to Frederick and then SR15 north to Thurmont. Take the SR77 exit ramp and turn right, to the west, for about three miles. Take a right into Park Central Road and immediately right into the Visitor Center of Catoctin Mountain Park. After the hike, use SR77 to get to Hagerstown to the lunch spot, which is just ½ mile from City Park where the art museum is located.

HOW LONG: The drive from the Beltway through Frederick to the park takes a little more than an hour. The hikes range from 30 minutes to all morning. The drive to the lunch place in Hagerstown takes about 30 minutes and is close to the art museum.

LUNCH BREAK: Casual dining is called for after a morning of hiking so try **Rik's Café** (1065 Maryland Ave., Hagerstown) for "classic sandwiches, hearty soups and crisp fun salads."

HIGHLIGHTS: **Catoctin Mountain Park** (administered by the National Park Service) and its twin across SR77, **Cunningham Falls State Park** (administered by Maryland), offer both a wealth of hiking trails through tall hardwood forests and fine blue-green vistas from their heights. The 78-foot cascading waterfall can be seen from both parks on separate boardwalk trails that are wheelchair accessible. It is hard to choose from the many interesting trails for a morning hike. A longish circular hike of about six miles that takes some three and a half hours goes from the Visitor Center to Cunningham Falls and then, after a steep climb upward, to Hog Rock at 1,610 feet before returning to the Visitor Center. If you want shorter hikes, go to Cunningham Falls and back from the Visitor Center (2.8 miles/two hours) or take round-trip hikes from parking lots along Park Central Road to reach Thurmont Vista (one mile, 45 minutes), Wolf Rock (1.8 miles, one and three-quarter hours), and an interpretative trail  telling the story of charcoal-making in the 1800s (one and a half miles, 30 minutes). Get a hiking map from the Visitor Center for these and other hikes.

The **Washington County Museum of Fine Arts** in Hagerstown's City Park has a well-rounded collection of Old Masters as well as traveling exhibitions of contemporary artists and, of course, the art of the museum's founder, William Henry Singer. An heir of Pittsburgh steel wealth, his painting was most inspired by the Norwegian landscape where he lived for years and collected paintings, sculptures, furniture, and decorative arts. Just around the corner from the art museum is **The Hager House**, the original home of the town's founder, who emigrated from Germany in 1736. He became a leading citizen and was elected to the General Assembly in Annapolis. The house has period furniture and herbal and flower gardens based on colonial varieties.

MORE INFORMATION

Catoctin Mountain
www.nps.gov/cato
6602 Foxville Road, Thurmont
301-663-9388
Open all year, daylight-dark
No entrance free
Download the NPS app for interactive maps,
amenities and more

Washington County Museum of Fine Arts
wcmfa.org
401 Museum Drive, City Park, Hagerstown
301-739-5727
Open Tuesday-Friday, 9am-5pm
Saturday, 9am-4pm
Sunday, 1-5pm
No entrance fee but contributions encouraged

The Hager House
hagerhouse.org
110 Key Street, City Park
301-739-8577 ext.170
Tours available by appointment; call 48 hours in
advance
Entrance fee $6/adult, $4/senior

Trip 8 – Biking through Antietam Battlefield and along the C&O Canal

WHY: Antietam (September 17, 1862) was the bloodiest one-day battle of the Civil War. The carnage of this scene, still palpable, is in strong contrast with the serene setting of the countryside and the green leafy C&O towpath just three miles away.

WHERE: Coming from Maryland or DC, go north on I-270 toward Frederick and take US40 Alt to Boonsboro and then SR34 west to Sharpsburg. The Antietam Visitor Center is north on SR65. Coming from Virginia, take SR7 and then SR9, until you reach Kearneysville. Turn northeast on WV SR480, which becomes MD SR34, to Sharpsburg where you turn north on SR65 to the Antietam Visitor Center.

HOW LONG: The trip to Antietam takes about one and a half hours. The circular bike trip around the Battlefield and along the C&O Canal and back is 21½ miles. The Visitor Center, the bike trip of the Battlefield, and the short trip to Shepherdstown takes about two hours. After lunch, the trip along the canal and back to the Visitor Center takes one and a half hours. The Battlefield Tour is very hilly, followed by the easy flat route along the river. However, the climb back up from the Potomac to the Visitor Center is strenuous.

LUNCH BREAK: **Blue Moon Cafe** (200 E. High Street) in downtown Shepherdstown has an "eclectic" menu and craft beers but is closed on Tuesday's. **Nutter's Ice Cream** (100 E. Main Street, Sharpsburg) on the way home is a good reward for a long cycling day.

HIGHLIGHTS: **Antietam Battlefield Tour** starts at the Visitor Center, which tells the story through exhibits and audio-visual programs of Lee's first foray onto Union soil and McClellan's inexcusable failure to follow him into Virginia. A year and a half into the Civil War, Union victory was far from assured. Lee's Maryland campaign was the most significant in a series of loosely coordinated Confederate incursions along a 1,000-mile front. Pick up a map of the automobile tour through the battlefield, which will be your bike route. Riding a bike gives you a better feel for the battle—the killing fields at the Dunker Church, Bloody Lane, and the cornfield—than an auto tour. The auto tour map shows clearly the 11 stops along the route, and the route is well-marked with many interpretive markers.

After stop #10, turn left onto Harpers Ferry Road and then right on Millers Sawmill Road, which takes you down to the **C&O Canal Towpath**. The towpath is well-suited for bikes, and the views are lovely and green. You can see some of the ruins of the old river locks. At **Shepherdstown** (West Virginia)**,** take the ramp up and cross the SR34 James Rumsey Bridge into town. Turn left on High Street for lunch at the **Blue Moon Café** (200 E. High St.) The town is known now for Shepherdstown College. The original land grant was in 1734. The town's walking tour points out that these old houses were filled with 3,000 wounded men after the battle at Antietam. After lunch, go back down to the towpath and ride for eight more scenic miles along the Potomac to Taylors Landing Boat Ramp. Cross the bridge and turn back on Bowie Road and then left on Mondell Road until you reach Dunker Church Road, which takes you back to the Antietam Visitor Center.

MORE INFORMATION

Antietam

> www.nps.gov/anti
> SR34, Sharpsburg
> 301-432-5124
> Open daily, 9am-5pm except Thanksgiving,
> Christmas, and New Year's Day
> Entrance fee $5/person, $10/vehicle

Shepherdstown Pedal and Paddle (for bike rental)
> 115 W. German Street, Shepherdstown
> 304-876-3000

Trip 9 – A Hike along the Appalachian Trail and an Afternoon in Frederick

WHY: For a pleasant morning's activity, you can't beat a walk in the woods along the Appalachian Trail to the nation's first monument to our First President, built by local citizens. A short distance by car is the town of Frederick where an elegant lunch awaits you beside Carrol Creek Linear Park followed by a unique museum dedicated to the challenges of Civil War Medicine.

WHERE: Take I-270 toward Frederick, turning on US40 Alt (Exit 49) toward Braddock Heights. In nine miles, park at the Old South Mountain Inn, cross the road, and get on the **Appalachian Trail** (white blazed) to the Washington Monument. Get back on US40 Alt to Frederick and continue to Carroll Creek at the river walk. Walk to the restaurant for lunch and then walk only minutes to the museum.

HOW LONG: It takes about 45 minutes to get from the Beltway to Old South Mountain Inn. The round-trip hike to the Washington Monument is a little over four miles. If you visit the little museum at the base of the trail and climb to the top of the monument, this can take about one and a half hours. The trip to the lunch spot in Frederick takes only a half hour and the museum is within walking distance from the restaurant.

LUNCH BREAK: **The Wine Kitchen on the Creek** (50 Carroll Creek Way) has an amazing farm fresh menu. We recommend the $15 lunch choices.

HIGHLIGHTS: **Washington Monument State Park** is a story of national pride. On July Fourth of 1827, most of Boonsboro's 500 residents assembled in the town square and, stepping briskly to the tunes of a fife and drum corps, marched the two miles up the mountain and completed the first 15 feet of the monument. By September it had risen to 30 feet. It was used by the Union Army as a signal tower during the Civil War. After falling into disrepair, it was completed in its present form by the Civilian Conservation Corps in 1936. It has sublime views of the valley below, especially in the fall. Most of the hiking trails in the park are part of the Appalachian National Scenic Trail.

Carroll Creek Linear Park: Carroll Creek occasionally flooded the surrounding part of the city of Frederick before 2007 when it was completely molded within reinforced banks to the tune of $60 million. The decaying buildings were torn down and the whole area gentrified. Today's visitors see a transformation—a lovely waterway in a 1.3-mile manmade channel with 40-foot-w i d e brick-lined, concrete banks. The promenade beside the creek is planted with trees and flowers and lined with shops, condos, and restaurants. Hundreds of water lilies cover the stream's surface. Strollers can cross three pedestrian bridges—including an unusual single-column suspension bridge—and several traffic bridges. The older spans include the hand-painted Community Bridge, a well-known piece of public art that has been Carroll Creek's main attraction since muralist William Cochran finished it in 1998.

National Museum of Civil War Medicine: A relatively new museum, the museum grew from the private collection of Dr. Gordon E. Damman. It consists of five immersion exhibits that recreate aspects of Civil War medical issues: life in an army camp, evacuation of the wounded from the battlefront, a field dressing station, a field hospital, and a military hospital ward. The exhibits incorporate surviving tools and equipment from the war, including the only known surviving Civil War surgeon's tent, surgical kits, and items pertaining to veterinary medicine. The museum's website invites you to "follow in the footsteps of soldiers and surgeons to discover the harsh conditions, personal sacrifices, and brilliant innovations of Civil War medicine, innovations that continue to save lives today."

MORE INFORMATION

Washington Monument State Park
 www.dnr.maryland.gov/publiclands/Pages/West
  ern/washington
 6620 Zittlestown Road, Middletown
 301-791-4767
 Open April-October, 8am-sunset
  and in the winter from 10am-sunset
 Museum open April-October weekends only,
  May-September, Thursday-Monday
 Entrance free

National Museum of Civil War Medicine
 www.civilwarmed.org/nmcwm/
 48 East Patrick Street, Frederick
 301-695-1864
 Open Monday, Thursday-Saturday 10am-5pm,
  Sunday 11am-5pm
 Entrance fee $9.50/adult, $8.50/senior

Trip 10 – An Easy Bike Ride along the C&O Canal to a Former Railroad Company Town

WHY: Brunswick, Maryland was once the site of the largest train yard in the country owned by one railroad (the B&O). Hitch a ride back in time and visit the museums that recount the glory days of both the C&O Canal and the B&O Railroads.

WHERE: From the Capital Beltway in Virginia, take Route 7 toward Leesburg. After 23 miles, turn north on US15. In 12 miles, you'll cross the Potomac River at Point of Rocks. Take the first road to the right, SR28, and then the first road to the left, Ballenger Creek Pike. Go up the hill and park in the lot of the Community Park on the right. Ride your bike down the hill and straight across the railroad tracks to get on the C&O canal towpath going north. In six miles, you'll be in Brunswick where you turn right across the tracks and up into town on Maple Avenue, turning left on West Potomac Street for the lunch stop that is only a few blocks away in an old church. After lunch, return along Potomac Street to the canal and train museum on the right.

HOW LONG: It takes about 40 minutes on a good day to get from Tyson's Corner to Leesburg and only 20 minutes to get to the bike park-out. Brunswick is less than an hour's bike ride away from that point, even with a few rest stops. After lunch, allot about an hour to visit both museums. After the hour bike ride back to Point of Rocks, the drive back to the Beltway should be less than an hour, particularly since the traffic flow in the afternoon is toward Maryland.

LUNCH BREAK: **Beans in the Belfry** (122 West Potomac Street) is a café located in a former 100-year-old church, complete with altar rails and stained glass windows. It serves imaginative sandwiches, hearty chili and quality teas and coffee. We had the chili and the Pangea Panini with prosciutto ham, brie, and sliced pears.

HIGHLIGHTS: The portion of the **C&O Canal Towpath** from Point of Rocks to Brunswick passes by several old lockkeepers' cottages with informative signage about life along the canal. It also includes the site of the Catoctin aqueduct, which has been recently restored by the Park Service with some of the original stones and ironwork. The aqueduct was vital to the transport system because it concurrently carried the canal and the railroad over Catoctin Creek, a Potomac tributary. Its original three arches collapsed during a storm in 1973 after 50 years of neglect.

In Brunswick, the **National Historical Park's Canal Museum** and the **Brunswick Heritage Museum** are in the same building. The first floor contains NHP's Visitor's Center and an exhibit of canal memorabilia and history. Learn what a thriving town Brunswick was and how cut-throat the competition was between the canals and the railroads. The second floor contains full sized reproductions of a railroader's life around 1900. The third floor is a spectacular HO-gauge model railroad, one of the largest on the east coast. Almost 1,000 feet of miniature track depict in amazing detail the key points along the B&O's five-mile route between Washington, DC and Brunswick from 1955 to 1965.

MORE INFORMATION

C&O Canal Visitor Center and **Brunswick Heritage Museum**

> www.canaltrust.org/pyv/brunswick-heritage-museum/
> 40 West Potomac Street, Brunswick
> 301-834-7100
> Open Saturday, 10am-4pm, Sunday, 1-4pm
> Entrance fee $7/adult

Beans in the Belfry

> Open Monday-Thursday, 8am-4pm
> Friday, 8am-9pm, weekends, 8am-6pm

C&O Canal Explorer Mobile App

The new app allows you to explore all 184.5 miles of the C&O Canal National Historical Park and features: 600 mapped and searchable points of interest, driving directions and mileage, and details about historic sites.

Trip 11 – A Hike on a Monadnock and a Visit to a Spectacular Museum on a Wooded Campus

WHY: On Sugarloaf Mountain you see beautiful uninterrupted views of the surrounding pastoral countryside all the way to Virginia. Then after eating your own packed lunch, wander through a man-made landscape at Glenstone contemporary art museum in Potomac.

WHERE: From the Capital Beltway, go north on I-270, turning off at the Hyattstown exit onto SR109 to Comus. Turn right on Comus Road to the entrance of the park. After hiking, get back on I-270 south, turning off toward the West on Sam Eig Highway in Gaithersburg and following your app's directions to Glenstone *if you have tickets*. If you do not have tickets, see box that advises you to take the bus to Glenstone from the Rockville metro station.

HOW LONG: From the Capital Beltway it takes about 45 minutes to get to Comus. An easy hike of about two hours on Sugarloaf followed by eating your own lunch there leaves a whole afternoon for getting to and wandering through Glenstone. Driving from Comus to the Rockville metro station takes about 30 minutes, and the bus takes about 35 minutes to get to Glenstone.

LUNCH BREAK: We could find no good lunch spots on the way to Glenstone. They were either fast foods or very expensive, such as the **Comus Inn** or the **Glenstone Café**, hence our advice to bring your own lunch.

HIGHLIGHTS: **Sugarloaf Mountain** is a monadnock, a mountain that remained after the erosion of the surrounding land, and it stands 800 feet above the surrounding farmland. Sugarloaf is administered by a nonprofit corporation and has been designated a Registered Natural Landmark because of its geological interest and beauty. Trail maps are available at each View Parking Lot. For a good two-hour hike over some rugged rocky areas, go to the West Parking lot and take the Green marked trail to the right of the shelter. It takes you to the summit of Sugarloaf among a forest of huge quartzite boulders and oak trees. On a clear day you can see way beyond the Potomac River to Leesburg. Take the marked trail to Bill Lambert's Overlook to see toward the Frederick side. Circle back on the blue and white-hashed trails to the West Parking lot.

Glenstone Museum is a private contemporary art museum founded in 2006 by a billionaire American businessman that draws from a collection of about 1,300 works from post-World War II artists around the world. The original building was designed by Charles Gwathmey, and it has been expanded several times on its 230-acre campus. Its most significant expansion was finished in 2018, with outdoor sculpture installations, landscaping, and an environmental center that has self-guided exhibits about recycling, composting and reforestation. The museum buildings are located toward the center of the campus, and visitors approach the galleries from gravel parking lots via a pathway through the property that is about one-third mile long. The founders were trying for a tranquil experience, leading art critics to refer to the museum as part of the "slow art" movement. To encourage the use of public transport, Glenstone successfully lobbied Montgomery County to add a bus stop near its campus and admits visitors without tickets who arrive on public buses (see information box).

MORE INFORMATION

Glenstone Museum
  www.glenstone.org/visit
  12100 Glen Rd., Potomac
  301-983-5001
  Open Thursday-Sunday, 10am-5pm
  Admission is always free, but it is nearly impossible
to get tickets online, and tickets are not available on site.
Guaranteed walk-in is offered to a large category of visitors
such as students (see the website), and passengers who
arrive at Glenstone on the Ride On bus (route 301). We
recommend the latter way to enter the museum, and the bus
route is online, with adequate parking available at the
Rockville station (parking costs $8.95 but bus is free to
seniors).

Trip 12 – Following the Patuxent from Howard to Prince George's County

WHY: Paddling the 800-acre Triadelphia Reservoir matches the tranquility of wilderness kayaking as no gas-powered engines are allowed and the shoreline is unblemished by human habitation. Go in the spring and enjoy the 20,000 azaleas at the dam. The reservoir's dam left the 1780s-built Montpelier Mansion high and dry above the Patuxent, but its 70 acres still allow one to imagine its former splendor.

WHERE: From the Capital Beltway, take Exit 31 north on Georgia Avenue (SR97) for about 13 miles. Turn right on Triadelphia Lake Road and go a short distance to a small parking lot at the boat launch. You can paddle your boat from here or just walk the mile-long Nature Trail (see box for how to get a single day use permit). After paddling, go back along Georgia Avenue and turn left on New Hampshire Road and then left on Brighton Dam Road. Continue to Clarksville for lunch. After lunch, take SR32 and turn east for about 20 miles until you reach the Baltimore-Washington Parkway (SR295). Turn right onto Laurel-Bowie Road (SR197), following signs to Montpelier Mansion. After your visit, retrace your route by turning south onto the B-W Parkway until you reach the Capital Beltway.

HOW LONG: The drive from the Beltway to the reservoir takes about a half hour. You can cover almost the entire reservoir in two hours of paddling. The drive after lunch to Montpelier takes only a half hour. An hour-long, self-guided tour of the Mansion and the grounds leaves time to explore the adjacent Montpelier Arts Center.

LUNCH BREAK: **Jinnie's Café and Deli** at Clarksville (6466 Ten Oaks Rd.); nothing fancy but tasty paninis, wraps and salads.

HIGHLIGHTS: The Washington Suburban Sanitary Commission's **Rocky Gorge and Triadelphia Reservoirs** provide both scenic beauty and a pure drinking supply for area residents. The two reservoirs hold 11 billion gallons of water. A full range of recreational activities is available, including shore and boat fishing, paddling, sailing, horsebacktrail riding, hunting, and walking, but the emphasis is on a quiet and clean environment. Many water birds find it an attractive space. The acclaimed **Brighton Dam Azalea Gardens** (blooms in May) has some 20,000 azaleas on five acres along the banks next to the dam.

    Montpelier Mansion in Laurel, now a national landmark, was built by Major Thomas Snowden and his wife Anne in the 1780s. He owned over 9,000 acres. Major Snowden fought in the American Revolution and was well connected both with Maryland's old families and with important government officials, including George Washington who "slept here" at least twice. After a succession of owners, Breckinridge Long, FDR's Undersecretary of State and US Ambassador to Italy in the 1930s, bought the house. His daughter donated it to the state in 1961. The house has been restored and furnished with antiques, including original Snowden pieces. The gift shop provides an excellent and free self-guided tour book. Next door in a reconstructed barn is the **Montpelier Arts Center**, a facility of area park commissions. Local artists have studios and show their works here.

MORE INFORMATION

Triadelphia Reservoir
www.wsscwater.com/watershedregs
2 Brighton Dam Road, Brookeville
301-774-9124
Boating permitted daily, March 15-November 30
from ½ hour before sunrise to sunset
Entrance fee $6/adult, $5.40/senior
Single day Watershed Use Permit $5 (boating)
Boating Permit can be bought at the Brighton Dam
Information Center, 2 Brighton Dam Road, from
March 1-December 15, 7am-8pm, or online at
www.WSSCwater.com

Montpelier Mansion
https://history.pgparks.com/3044/
Montpelier-house-museum
650 Muirkirk Road, Laurel
301-377-7817
Self-guided tours year-round, Thursday-Monday,
10am-3pm, closed Tuesday-Wednesday
Entrance fee $5/adult, $4/senior

Montpelier Arts Center
www.pgparks.com/Our_Facilities/
Montpelier_Arts_Center
9652 Muirkirk Road
301-377-7800
Open daily, 10am-5pm
Entrance free

Trip 13 – Hiking Patapsco River Valley and Exploring its History

WHY: A 32-mile-long green oasis halfway between DC and Baltimore is now a mecca for hikers, equestrians, mountain bikers, and fly fishermen but is also an area important in the history of the railroads, especially during the Civil War.

WHERE: From the Capital Beltway, take I-95 north to Exit 47, I-195 east. Turn off at Exit 3 toward Elkridge (US1 south), taking the next right onto South Street. The park entrance is immediately on the left. Pay the entrance fee and buy a hiking map. Drive a couple of miles into the park, turning left at a dead end and then continuing to a parking lot near the restrooms and across from the swinging bridge. After the hike, retrace your steps to I-95 south and turn west onto SR100. In two miles, exit onto Snowdon River Parkway and then immediately west on SR108. Take the first right onto Richards Valley Road to the Coal Fire restaurant. After lunch, continue on SR108 to Ellicott City to the B&O Railroad Museum. After a tour of the museum and the town, go back to the Beltway and home.

HOW LONG: It takes about a half hour from the Beltway to reach Patapsco Valley State Park. The five-mile hike took us two and a half hours. The ride to lunch is only 20 minutes, and you can spend a few hours exploring Ellicott City shops and touring the Railroad Museum.

LUNCH BREAK: You can wait to get to Ellicott City for a large selection of restaurants on Main Street or eat along the way at **Coal Fire Pizza** (5725 Richards Valley Road). With a thin crust just like in Italy and fresh ingredients made on the premises, it has a lot to recommend it.

HIGHLIGHTS: **Patapsco Valley State Park** encompasses more than 16,000 acres and eight areas and is nationally known for its trail opportunities (170 miles' worth) and scenery. This hike is in the Orange Grove area at the southern end that was once the home of the village of Orange Grove, a mill town that thrived in the 1800s. You can visit the site across a swinging bridge similar to the one that spanned the river back then. The hike begins at the "Cascade Falls Trail" sign up the hill from the parking area. You need the hiking map from the entrance station, or you will get lost on the well-marked but bewildering number of trails. We took a circular route—the blue-blazed Cascade Falls Trail, the yellow-blazed Morning Choice Trail, and the orange-blazed Ridge Trail. There is always something of interest—a series of falls tumbling toward the Patapsco River, ruins of houses abandoned by the mill workers, and the thick canopy of beech and maple. Spanning the park road almost at the entrance is the 175-year-old Thomas Viaduct, the oldest major railroad viaduct in North America and the first built on a curve.

The **B&O Railroad Museum at the Elliott City Station** is the oldest railroad station in America. When it opened in 1831, railroad trains were still drawn by horses. The station recreates a working station and houses an HO-gauge model train layout of the first thirteen miles of the B&O railroad. A video explains its strategic importance during the Civil War. The historic center of **Ellicott City**, founded in 1772 as a mill town, is a charming and interesting spot.

MORE INFORMATION

Patapsco Valley State Park
  www.dnr.state.md.us/publiclands/central/patapsco
  8020 Baltimore National Pike, Ellicott City
  410-461-5005
  Open year-round, daily, 9am-sunset
  Good trail maps can be found on the website
  Entrance free for seniors over 62
    Weekdays, in-state $2/adult, out of state $4/adult
    Weekends, in state $3/adult, out of state $5/adult

B&O Railroad Museum: Ellicott City Station
  ellicottcity.net/Tourism/attractions/bo_railroad_
    museums_ellicott_city_station/
  3711Maryland Avenue, Ellicott City
  410-313-1945
  Open Wednesday-Thursday, 10am-3pm
    Friday-Sunday, 10am-5pm
    Closed Monday and Tuesday
  Entrance free

Trip 14 – Biking Patapsco River Valley and Decoding the Cryptologic Museum

WHY: Both sights are historically important—a once thriving industrial riverside that is now a verdant state park and a nearby museum that chronicles how codes and ciphers have shaped US history.

WHERE: From the Capital Beltway, take I-95 north to Exit 47, I-195 east. Turn off at Exit 3 toward Elkridge (US1 south), taking the next right onto South Street. The park entrance is immediately on the left. At the dead end, turn right and park in the parking lot on the right. See directions for the bike ride in the Information Box. After your biking, return to US1 where you will turn right, and in about four miles turn left on SR103 and then left on Dorsey Road for lunch. To reach the museum, get on the B&W Parkway south (SR295) exiting on SR32 east and follow the signs to the Cryptologic Museum off Canine Road. To go home, get on SR32 toward Columbia and exit on the GW Parkway toward Washington.

HOW LONG: It takes about a half hour from the Beltway to reach Patapsco Valley State Park. The 10-mile bike trip took us about one and a half hours. Lunch was only 10 minutes away and the museum 15 minutes from there. The docent-led tour took about 45 minutes, but you can spend additional time on your own. When leaving, the Beltway is about 12 minutes from the museum.

LUNCH BREAK: The **Stained Glass Pub** (6751 Dorsey Road) in Elkridge is the only eating establishment in the area with good reviews, and it turned out to be a popular spot.

HIGHLIGHTS: **Patapsco Valley State Park** has one of the most extensive trail networks in the Maryland state park system for hikers, mountain bikes, and touring bikes. Its two hanging bridges provide unique views of the valley. The vegetation is thick and lush, and you are never far from the clear meandering stream that was once the mighty Patapsco. This river turned the turbines of the country's first submerged hydroelectric dam and supplied the water for a thriving riverside business community that included a forge, grist mill, and nail factory. The nation's first railroad tracks, belonging to the Baltimore and Ohio (B&O), provided transport for these businesses and still hang precipitously above the river. The early residents of an area that had such economic promise  would surely be astonished at how present-day visitors must search for signs of past human habitation. The Avalon Visitor Center features exhibits spanning 300 years of history along the river.

The **National Cryptologic Museum** houses the nation's priceless collection of cryptologic artifacts and is the only public museum in the Intelligence Community. It is adjacent to the National Security Agency Headquarters. Here visitors can learn about some of the most dramatic moments in the history of American cryptology, the people who devoted their lives to it, and the machines and devices that helped them fulfill their mission. The extensive reference library is open to the public. It has a large collection of commercial codebooks, unclassified monographs, and the first printed book on cryptology (1518), strangely enough, by a German mystic. The book was a gift of the leading historian of cryptology, David Kahn, author of *The Codebreakers*. Try to catch a docent-led tour or take an audio tour with your cell phone. Specialized tours focus on American Cryptologic History (60-90 minutes), Women in Cryptology (60 minutes) and Advancing Technologies (60 minutes).

MORE INFORMATION

Patapsco Valley State Park
> www.dnr.state.md.us/publiclands/central/patapsco
> 8020 Baltimore National Pike, Ellicott City
> 410-461-5005
> Open year-round, daily, 9am-sunset
> Good trail maps can be found on the website
> Entrance free for seniors over 62
>> Weekdays, in-state $2/adult, out of state $4/adult
>> Weekends, in state $3/adult, out of state $5/adult

Directions for Bike Ride: From the parking lot, go back to the main road and follow it until you come to the swinging bridge. Cross it, go left on the Grist Mill Trail and follow River Road after leaving the park until it merges with Frederick Road. Turn around and go back straight along the trail, around the lake, and back to the parking lot.

National Cryptologic Museum
> www.nsa.gov/about/cryptologic-heritage/museum
> 8290 Colony Seven Road, Ft. George G. Meade
> 301-688-5849
> Open Tuesday, Thursday-Saturday, 10am-4pm
>> Wednesday, 10am-7pm, closed Monday
> Entrance free

Trip 15 – Biking from Columbia to Savage Mill: Suburban Sprawl to Suburban Small

WHY: You won't find any more fun bicycle ride than the four and a half-mile stretch between Columbia and Savage Mill, weaving its way on multiple boardwalks and bridges along and over the Patuxent Branch. Then you can lunch and shop at Historic Savage Mill on the site of an 1820s textile weaving business before heading back on the bike trail.

WHERE: From the Capital Beltway, take I-95 North toward Baltimore for 11 miles and take SR32 West to Broken Land Parkway. Go north toward Owen Brown. Turn right on Cradlerock Way, right on Dockside Lane, and then immediately left into the parking lot at Lake Elkhorn. Begin biking toward the right and soon you will see signs to the Patuxent Branch Trail. In four and a half miles, the trail ends at Savage Park. Exit the park, turning left on Washington Street until you come to the Mill complex. After your visit, go back to Lake Elkhorn via the Patuxent Branch Trail and then drive to I-95 via SR32.

HOW LONG: From the Beltway, it takes no more than 20 minutes to get to Lake Elkhorn in Columbia. The Patuxent Branch Trail to Savage can take one and a half hours if you do the loop around the lake in Columbia first. Lunch and shop at your leisure at Historic Savage Mill. Then you can take the two-mile up and back trip along the Savage Historic Mill Trail before heading back. If you do that, the return trip to the Lake should take one and a half hours.

LUNCH BREAK: There are several good places to eat in Historic Savage Mill. We recommend **Dive Bar and Grill** or you can just grab a sandwich at the more casual **Bonaparte Breads and Café**.

HIGHLIGHTS: **Patuxent Branch Trail** is part of a 20-mile trail system that follows a former B&O Railroad line along the Patuxent River. Ten bridges raise you above the flood plain. You ride through thick forest, only occasionally mindful of the highways far above that carry continual heavy traffic. The most impressive bridge is the Guilford-Pratt Truss Bridge. Signs along the rail explain the historical significance of Howard County's two main industries—the railroad and the granite quarry. You bike straight through the latter, which operated until 1928.

Historic **Savage Mill** is the site of an old textile mill on the banks of the Little Patuxent River, which operated from 1822 to 1947. The water from the river flowed over a huge 30-foot water wheel that powered the textile machinery. The main product was canvas, used to make sails for Baltimore's clipper ships, cannon covers, and other supplies for the Civil War, and even painted backdrops for Hollywood's first silent movies. The Mill buildings now house over 30 eclectic businesses that include a huge antique mall and craft studios and galleries that will keep you shopping for hours. Before you head back on the trail, take the short (one mile each way) **Savage Mill Trail** that starts at the old Bollman Truss Bridge. There were originally 100 of these handsome iron structures built for the B&O Railroad, but this is the only one left. Part of the railroad tracks have been left for atmosphere. The trail is mostly paved and flat along the river, but there is some gravel and dirt before it dead ends in the forest.

Trip 16 – Views of the Potomac from Great Falls Tavern Trails and Clara Barton's Home

WHY: The famous Section A of the Billy Goat Trail on the Maryland side of Great Falls is too challenging for many hikers, but the overlook from Olmstead Island provides striking views of the falls with less stress on the body. Downriver, Clara Barton, founder of the Red Cross, enjoyed panoramic views of the Potomac from her perch in Glen Echo.

WHERE: From the Capital Beltway, take Exit 41 (the Clara Barton Parkway) toward Glen Echo. Directions to the Clara Barton National Historic Site are clearly marked. Go off the Parkway toward Cabin John, turning right on MacArthur Blvd. and then right onto Oxford Road. For lunch, you have two choices: either north or south on MacArthur Blvd. for very short distances. After lunch, get back on the Clara Barton Parkway and go north, turning off at the second exit (marked Carderock), and driving to the parking lot of the Great Falls Tavern on MacArthur Blvd. After hiking, retrace your steps to the Beltway.

HOW LONG: This is easy driving from the Beltway—nothing more than 10 minutes away. The Park Service tour at the Clara Barton house takes 45 minutes, and you might want to walk next door for a few minutes to see Glen Echo Park, another historic site. The hike to and from the falls from Great Falls Tavern takes about ¾ hour.

LUNCH BREAK: Next door to Glen Echo Park just off MacArthur Blvd. is the **Irish Inn at Glen Echo** (6119 Tulane Avenue). Aptly describing itself as "upscale casual," it serves good Shepherd's Pie, fish and chips, and fish tacos. Up the road in Cabin John, the **Market on the Boulevard** (7945 MacArthur

Blvd.) serves tasty sandwiches imaginatively named, such as the "Clara Barton" and the "C&O Canal."

HIGHLIGHTS: The **Clara Barton National Historic Site** provides a fascinating insight into the life of this humanitarian. Born in 1821, she was first a teacher, then worked at the US Patent Office, and finally found her life's work during the Civil War, saying, "If I can't be a soldier, I'll help soldiers." She solicited donations of supplies, nursed the wounded on the battlefield, and wrote letters to soldiers' families. After the war, during a visit to Europe, she learned about the International Red Cross, established after the signing of the Geneva Convention. After a long struggle, she founded the American Red Cross and served as its president from 1881 to 1904. The site in Glen Echo was given to the Red Cross by local entrepreneurs who wanted to promote their new town and the establishment of a Chautauqua, a concept whose aim was to bring education and culture to the masses. The house was built as a giant warehouse for disaster supplies with dormitory space for Red Cross volunteers and a few rooms for her personal use. The remnants of the Chautauqua next door are now **Glen Echo Park** where the National Park hosts a variety of activities.

The view from the Olmstead Island overlook of the **C&O Canal National Historic Park** is breathtaking; the short trail starts at the Great Falls Tavern Visitor Center. You might be treated to watching daredevil kayakers trying to get to the bottom of the falls in one piece. Hike, if you must, Section A of the Billy Goat Trail (sign clearly marked) but there are also easier Sections B and C although they do not have views of the falls. Back at the Tavern Visitor's Center, you can ride a canal boat pulled by mules, the original power source, for about a mile out and back, a good way to observe the working of the locks on the C&O canal that eventually reached Georgetown.

MORE INFORMATION

Clara Barton National Historic Site
 www.nps.gov/clba
 5801 Oxford Road, Glen Echo
 301-320-1400
 Guided tours only; Friday, Saturday, Sunday at
  1pm, 2pm, 3pm and 4pm, first floor only
 Entrance free

Glen Echo Park
 www.glenechopark.org
 7300 MacArthur Blvd., Glen Echo
 301-634-2222

C&O Canal National Historic Park
 www.nps.gov/choh/index.htm
 Hiking maps:
 www.nps.gov/choh/planyourvisit/upload/Great-
  Falls-Hiking-Map.pdf

Visitor Center – Great Falls Tavern
 11710 MacArthur Blvd., Potomac
 301-767-3714
 Open during daylight hours except Monday and
  Tuesday
 Admission $20 per vehicle

Trip 17 – Boating and Hiking in Patuxent River Park

WHY: From its source at Parris Ridge in Carroll County to its mouth at Drum Point on the Chesapeake Bay—110 miles—the Patuxent River is known for its natural beauty and is one of Maryland's Scenic Rivers. This trip explores its rich marshlands area.

WHERE: From the Capital Beltway, take Exit 11A, Pennsylvania Avenue (SR4), and go eight miles. Take US301 south and go 3.6 miles, turning onto Croom Road (SR382) and then turning left onto Croom Airport Road to the park driveway.

HOW LONG: The drive takes about three-quarters of an hour from the Beltway. You can spend a leisurely day here—boating on the river, visiting Mount Calvert Historical and Archaeological Park and the Rural Life Museum, and hiking on the trails and boardwalks.

LUNCH BREAK: There are no restaurants in or near the Park. We bought a deli sandwich at **Safeway** (on US301 before turning onto Croom Road) and ate it under a tree overlooking Jug Bay from Mount Calvert. Take plenty of liquids with you.

HIGHLIGHTS: **Patuxent River Park** is only a small part of the area protected by the Patuxent River Watershed Act. It is Stop 47 along the Patuxent Water Trail, which offers visitors a chance to paddle the whole river and camp along its banks. We put in our kayak at Jug Bay Natural Area (Jackson's Landing), which is near park headquarters and where you can rent canoes. You can paddle in either direction to get a good taste of the rich marsh habitat but plan your trip for high tide or risk getting mired in the soft mud and weeds. We saw nesting ospreys and both mature and young bald eagles. Profuse purple pickerel weed festoons the marsh during June and July. Take bug spray. If you don't want to boat, there are eight miles of scenic woodland trails for hikers and bicyclists. The marshes are a critical stopover point for migrating soras (a type of bird species known as rails) that are travelling from their breeding grounds in New England and eastern Canada to their winter homes further south. After fattening up here, they can make non-stop fall flights of 500 miles.

You can paddle to Stop 44 or drive (off Croom Airport Road) to **Mount Calvert Historical and Archaeological Park**. It is "a confluence of three cultures" because the site represents 8,000 years of American Indian, Euro-American, and African American life. In 1684, it was named Mount Calvert, and it became Prince George's first county seat, then named Charles Town. In 1696, the county seat moved to Upper Marlboro and Mount Calvert reverted to a typical southern Maryland plantation. The existing federal period house was built in 1789 on a high knoll that marks the joining of the Patuxent and its West Branch. An ongoing archaeological dig is uncovering the town's buildings, and the archaeologists are eager to show off their discoveries. A small museum in the house tells the site's long story in an interesting way. It is open only on the weekends, but if the archaeologists are on-site, you can peek inside on weekdays. Back at Park Headquarters at Jug Bay, a short trail leads to the **Rural Life Museum**. It is open weekends to the public and features antique farm and kitchen implements, a catalog-sold Sears house, a log cabin built in 1864 by a former slave, and an informative exhibit on Maryland tobacco. A new addition to the park is **The American Indian Village** that replicates an Eastern Woodland Village.

MORE INFORMATION

Patuxent River Park
   www.pgparks.com/Things To Do/Nature/Patuxent
      River_Park.htm
   16000 Croom Airport Road, Upper Marlboro
   301-627-6074
   Open daily, 8am-sunset
      Visitor Center open 8am-4pm
   Water Trail access closes January-March
   Entrance free

Mount Calvert Historical and Archaeological Park
   www.pgparks.com/facilities/facility/details/Mount-
   Calvert-Historical-and-Archaeologi-260
   16801 Mount Calvert Road, Upper Marlboro
   301-627-1286
   House and museum open Saturday, 10am-4pm
      Sunday, noon-4pm
   Archaeological excavations open most Saturdays
   Entrance free

Trip 18 – Bike Trip around Piscataway Park with a Stop at the National Harbor

WHY: This bike trip offers a surprisingly unobstructed view of Mount Vernon across the river from the recreated old tobacco farm in Piscataway Park, and a short drive away is the burgeoning Potomac-front development known as the National Harbor.

WHERE: Take Indian Head Highway (SR210) south off the Capital Beltway. Go 10 miles to the intersection in Accokeek, turning right on Livingston Road (at B&J Carryout). Start biking at the fire station, which is on the right about three quarters of a mile from the turnoff (you will have already seen signage to Piscataway National Park). After biking, drive back Indian Head Highway to the Beltway heading toward Virginia to the well-marked exits to the National Harbor.

HOW LONG: The 10-mile circular bike trip is an easy one, with a midway rest stop at Piscataway National Park. The bike trip plus a tour of the Colonial Farm takes about two and a half hours. After lunch, tour National Harbor at your leisure.

LUNCH BREAK: We were too starved to wait until we arrived at the National Harbor for lunch, so we stopped at **B&J Carryout** (15805 Livingston Road in Accokeek) for "Dixie-Style BarBQ"-- finely chopped pork with a sweet pickle/coleslaw relish. Also on the menu are soft shell crab and oyster sandwiches. If you can wait to eat until you reach National Harbor, the choices are endless, from casual to very fancy.

HIGHLIGHTS: The bike ride along quiet country roads from your parking place at the fire station takes you to **Piscataway National Park**. The Accokeek Foundation stewards 200 pristine acres of Piscataway Park's woodlands, fields and waterfront along the Potomac. The **National Colonial Farm** there lets you experience what life was like for a typical tobacco-planting family in Prince George's County in the 1770s. It includes a tobacco-drying barn, rare-breed heritage animals, and authentic crops of the time. You can hike and walk the boardwalks over freshwater tidal wetlands, fish off the pier while viewing Mount Vernon across the river, bird watch from bird observation blinds, or launch your boat or kayak from the shore. Leaving the park, follow Cactus Hill Road and Old Marshall Hall Road back to the firehouse.

After lunch, on your way home, stop at the 300-acre **National Harbor**—within a stone's throw of the Wilson Bridge. Its 15th anniversary was only in 2023. The giant rising out of the ground at the waterfront ("The Awakening"), was moved there from Haines Point. National Harbor boasts shops, restaurants, a venue for concerts and shows, a giant carousel with enclosed gondolas rising 180 ft. above the harbor ($17 per person), and kayaks and pedal boats to rent. The Gaylord Hotel offers its guests a dinner cruise. Water taxis are available to and from Alexandria.

MORE INFORMATION

Piscataway Park
> www.nps.gov/pisc
> 13551 Fort Washington Road, Fort Washington
> 301-763-4600
> Open March 1-November 30,
>> Tuesday-Saturday, 10am-4pm
>> December 1-February 28, weekends only,
>> 10am-4pm
>
> Entrance free

National Colonial Farm
> 301-283-2113
> Open March to December, Tuesday-Sunday,
>> 10am-4pm
>
> Entrance free but fees for programmed activities

National Harbor
> www.nationalharbor.com

Trip 19 – Biking through History in Charles County

WHY: Charles Country was created in 1658 as a royal colony by Charles Calvert, 3rd Lord Baltimore, and has some of the oldest historic sites in the state. As it is still beyond the reach of the DC area commute, it is unspoiled beyond the US301 corridor, with a sparsely populated shoreline along the Potomac River.

WHERE: Take SR5 (Exit 7) off the Capital Beltway toward Waldorf. Follow US301when SR5 turns off toward St. Mary's County. Turn right on SR488 and follow the signs to Port Tobacco. Leave your car in the parking lot at the old Port Tobacco Courthouse. The entire bike tour is a figure eight that is 28 miles round-trip. If you want a shorter, circular trip, park somewhere in La Plata and take only the first part of the tour by bike, finishing it at your car.

HOW LONG: The drive south to Port Tobacco takes about three quarters of an hour. Each 14-mile segment of the bike ride takes about two hours. You'll still have time to explore old Port Tobacco, Saint Ignatius Church, and the Thomas Stone House.

LUNCH BREAK: La Plata, Charles County's county seat, is the only place along the route to have lunch. **The Greene Turtle** (6 St. Mary's Avenue) has a typical sports bar menu (hearty sandwiches and burgers).

HIGHLIGHTS: The bike trip goes past five historic sites, starting with old **Port Tobacco**, which was colonized by the English in 1634 and became the second largest river port in Maryland. It became a ghost town after silt and tidal action cut if off from the sea and the county seat moved to La Plata. The former courthouse has been rebuilt as a tiny historical museum and furnished as a nineteenth century courtroom with exhibits on tobacco and archaeological finds. **St. Ignatius Catholic Church**, founded in 1641 by the Jesuits, is the oldest continuously active parish in the US. It has magnificent views of the Potomac River from its high bluff.

After lunch in La Plata, ride past **Mt. Carmel Monastery**, the first convent in America, founded in 1790 by Carmelite nuns. The buildings were restored in 1935 and can be viewed from the outside only. The **Thomas Stone House**, Haber de Venture, was built in 1773 and is a National Historic Site. It has a National Park Visitors Center that offers information, exhibits, and tours. Stone, a lawyer and planter, was one of the four Maryland signers of the Declaration of Independence. **Rose Hill**, built in the late eighteenth century and restored in 1937, was the home of Dr. Gustavus Brown, a friend of George Washington and an attending physician at his death. It was later the home of Olivia Floyd, a Confederate agent. The house is in private hands today and can only be seen from the road when the leaves are off the trees. Google "The Legend of the Blue Dog of Rose Hill" for a ghost story.

Directions for Bike Ride:
START at Port Tobacco Courthouse on Chapel Point Road
Continue on Chapel Point Road to St. Ignatius Church
Cross US301 onto Bel Alton Newtown Road
Left on Springhill Newtown Road
Right on Glen Albin Road, turn Right on St. Mary's Ave. for lunch
Right on SR 6 and then immediately left on Washington Avenue
Left on Mitchell Road and cross US301
Detour Left on Mt. Carmel Road to see Monastery on Hawthorne Road (SR225)
Left on Rose Hill Road to Thomas Stone House and Rose Hill
Left on SR6 and then right on Chapel Point Road to return to parking lot

MORE INFORMATION

Port Tobacco Historic Village
> www.charlescountymd.gov/locations/port-
> tobacco-courthouse
> 8190 Port Tobacco Rd.
> 301-392-3418
> Daily tours that include the Port Tobacco
> Courthouse, Stagg Hall, and Burch House
> April-December, Thursday-Sunday, 10am-4pm

Thomas Stone House: www.nps.gov/thst
> 6655 Rose Hill Road, Port Tobacco
> 801-761-9263
> Open April-December, Thursday-Sunday, 10am-4pm
> Entrance free

Up the Creek Rentals (bike rental)
> www.upthecreekrentals.net
> 108 Mattingly Avenue, Indian Head
> 301-743-3733

View from St. Ignatius Catholic Church

Trip 20 – Remnants of Two Wars: Mallows Bay in Charles County and Fort Washington in Prince George's County

WHY: A paddle in Mallows Bay around the carcasses of sunken cargo ships used in WWI allows access to a small creek that hosts large numbers of eagles and ospreys [for those without kayaks, see box]. Then drive further north to Fort Washington, an impressive fortification that was built when England was our most feared enemy.

WHERE: From the Capital Beltway, take Exit 3 south—Indian Head Highway, which is SR210. Turn left onto Bryans Road (SR227), which merges into SR224. In about 12 miles, turn right on Wilson Landing Road to Mallows Bay Park. For lunch, retrace your steps to the junction with SR210. After lunch, continue back along SR210, turning left onto Fort Washington Road.

HOW LONG: From the Beltway exit, the drive to Mallows Bay takes under 45 minutes. Paddle for a couple of hours and then head for lunch at Accokeek. Exploring nearby Fort Washington takes about an hour but more if you are a military history buff.

LUNCH BREAK: Eateries are modest in this area, so we repeat a previously recommended spot **B&J Carryout** (15805 Livingston Road and Indian Head Highway) in Accokeek. Both the barbecue and seafood choices are delicious as well as the ice cream.

HIGHLIGHTS: **Mallows Bay Park** in Charles County is the sunken graveyard of more than 230 ships, the largest such graveyard in the Western Hemisphere. Ninety were poorly constructed steamships built during World War I, and in 1925 they were burned and scuttled in the Bay. During World War II,

Bethlehem Steel built a salvage basin there to recover the metal. All that is left now are rotting timbers and huge nail-heads protruding eerily out of the water, a "ghost fleet." Mallows Bay was declared a National Marine Sanctuary in 2019. The carcasses of the ships have attracted water birds to build their nests, and at high tide, you can kayak way back into the bay to see more ospreys and eagles. We guarantee that you will see few humans if you go during the week. The park has a nice kayak launch.

Fort Washington Park, a National Park Service site, illustrates changing military strategies, technology, and enemies. The first fort can be considered a failure. During the War of 1812, the British marched overland and burned Washington. British ships then sailed up the Potomac, and the fort was blown up to keep it from falling into British hands. A new fort rose from its ashes as the outer defense for the Nation's Capital. Prior to WWI, the Fort was downgraded to harbor defense and the big guns removed, becoming a staging area for moving troops to France. It is now a ceremonial site for the Military District of Washington. Pick up a brochure at the Visitor Center (the yellow house) for a good self-guided tour.

MORE INFORMATION

Mallows Bay Park

    www.charlescountyparks.com
    1440 Wilson Landing Road, Nanjemoy
    301-932-3470
    Open year-round, daily, 5:30am-dusk
    Entrance and boat launch free
    Water Trail map available on website
    Guided tours with rental kayaks are offered by
        Charles County Recreation, Parks, and Tourism:
        www.charlescountyparks.com/parks/

Fort Washington Park

    www.nps.gov/fowa
    13551 Fort Washington Road, Fort Washington
    301-763-4600
    Park grounds open daily, 7am-sunset
    Visitors Center and Historic Fort open Thursday-
        Sunday, 9am-4:30pm
    Entrance free

Trip 21 – Two Boardwalks: One over a Swamp and the other over an Abandoned Railway

WHY: Calvert County is full of surprises. From a boardwalk, see the primeval beauty of a swamp that is the vestigial remains of a vast swamp 100,000 years ago. Then walk along another boardwalk over an abandoned railroad corridor in Chesapeake Beach and visit its first-rate railway museum that also tells the Town's origin story.

WHERE: At Capital Beltway exit 11A, take SR4 south. After about 30 miles and going past Prince Frederick, turn right onto State Route 506 and then Grays Rd. to reach Battle Creek Cypress Swamp. Get back on SR4 heading north and turn right on SR263 and then SR261 to Chesapeake Beach. Return on SR260, following signs to DC and the Beltway.

HOW LONG: It takes about 50 minutes from the Beltway to Battlefield Cypress Swamp and a half hour to get to Chesapeake Beach. Another half hour gets you back to the Beltway.

LUNCH BREAK: Near the Railway Museum in Chesapeake Beach (4165 Mears Ave.) is the **Boardwalk Café**. It isn't fancy but it has good pizzas, pitas and calzones.

HIGHLIGHTS: **Battle Creek Cyprus Swamp Sanctuary** lies in 100 acres saved by the Nature Conservancy. This is the northernmost limit in the US of the bald cypress, which was common 100,000 years ago. Walk the quarter-mile boardwalk trail and marvel at the 100-foot canopy of these trees and their characteristic knobby "knees." Why the knees exist is still an unsolved mystery—are they snorkels, or do they provide stability in the mucky habitat? Watch for turtles and frogs.

Chesapeake Beach Railway Museum remembers the grand vision of a Russian immigrant who built a huge resort town on the Bay as well as a railway to carry visitors from Washington and Baltimore. It opened in 1900 and folded in the mid-1930s, a victim of the Great Depression and the increasing popularity of the automobile. It was colossal for its time and included beachfront hotels, a racetrack, casino, beaches with bathhouses, a 1600-foot boardwalk, band shell, and an amusement park. The boardwalk and amusement park were built out over the water. A mile-long pier—so long because of the shallow Bay—was built to receive passengers arriving daily by steamer from Baltimore. The museum has interesting photos and artifacts as well as an audio-visual presentation of the history. All that is left today are the rotting pilings, but they give a hint of how large the project was. Now, along the same shore, attractive condos, hotels, and restaurants crowd the waterfront. A short distance north is North Beach, with its 1920s style cottages protected by a new seawall.

Chesapeake Beach Railway Trail is a boardwalk 1.4 miles long that occupies a portion of the abandoned railroad corridor that whisked vacationers from DC to the grand hotels, beaches and boardwalk of Chesapeake Beach. Now it offers panoramic views of the surrounding marshland, forest and Fishing Creek.

MORE INFORMATION

Battle Creek Cypress Swamp Sanctuary
> www.calvertcountymd.gov/1505/Park-Hours
> 2880 Gray's Road, Prince Frederick
> 410-535-5327
> Open daily, Monday-Friday, 9am-4:30pm
> > Saturday, 10am-6pm
> > Sunday, 1pm-6pm
> Slightly shorter hours Labor Day-Memorial Day
> Entrance free

Chesapeake Beach Railway Museum
> cbrailway@calvertcountymd.gov
> 4155 Mears Avenue, Chesapeake Beach
> 410-257-3892
> Open daily, April-October 31, 1pm-4pm
> Entrance free

Chesapeake Beach Railway Trail
> www.traillink.com/trail-maps/chesapeake-
> > railway-trail
> Parking can be found at the Chesapeake Beach
> > Water Park on Gordon Stinnett Blvd.

Trip 22 – A Hike on the Watery Side in Calvert County

WHY: Ten million years ago, Calvert County was a watery world of whales and sharks, the fossil remains of which you can find today at Flag Ponds Nature Park. That history and the county's water-based economy are expertly documented in the Calvert Marine Museum. Nearby Annmarie Garden provides a whimsical blend of art and nature.

WHERE: At Capital Beltway Exit 11A, take SR4 south into Calvert County. About 10 miles south of Prince Frederick, turn left into Flag Ponds Nature Park. Solomon's Island is about 10 miles further on State Routes 2/4 (joint here). Go past the Marine Museum on Solomon's Island Road and turn left at the lunch spot on C Street. After lunch, go back and visit the Marine Museum and then go north on SR2/4 out of Solomon's, turning right onto Dowell Road into Annmarie Garden.

HOW LONG: The drive to Flag Pond takes about 40 minutes from the Beltway. Spend the morning on the beach and drive the 10 minutes or so to Solomon's for lunch. After lunch, tour the Marine Museum, worth a couple of hours, and walk through the Annmarie Sculpture Garden and Arts Center for another hour.

LUNCH BREAK: Solomon's Island has a large collection of seafood restaurants. Try **Zahniser's Dry Dock** (251 C Street). It has both steak and seafood with harbor views.

HIGHLIGHTS: **Flag Ponds Nature Park** occupies land that was once a sheltered harbor on the Chesapeake Bay supporting a "pound net" fishing operation that supplied croaker, trout, and herring to city markets. You can see the one remaining shanty that housed fishermen during the fishing season furnished as it once was. Take the half-mile trail to the beach, and you step back in time to the remains of a primordial sea. Download a trail map.

Sharp-eyed visitors can spot sharks' teeth and other Miocene fossils along the shell-strewn shoreline. The beach is very clean, and people are few and far between because of its lack of car access. There are other trails to small freshwater ponds where you can see turtles, sea birds, and ducks. <u>Take bug spray, sunscreen, and water</u>. When you hike back to the Visitor Center, compare your finds with the displays of marine fossils that others have found.

The **Calvert Marine Museum** is a gem (see their video if you don't believe us), appealing to all ages. The wonders of prehistoric times are in exhibits displaying the skeletons of scary sea creatures, a visual diary of the recent find of an ancient whale in Calvert Cliffs and a time lapse video of the Chesapeake as the seas ebbed and  flowed. The artifacts of the area's fishing industry are equally fascinating and well presented, with the moved and restored Drum Point Lighthouse dominating the Museum's waterfront. It is furnished just as the last lighthouse keeper and his family left it. Add to this real live fish, crabs, and otters, and you have an entertaining afternoon.

Annmarie Garden Sculpture Park, a gift from a local benefactor to the county in 1991, features a shaded walking path that meanders past permanent and loaned works of outdoor sculpture, many from the Smithsonian's Hirshhorn collection. A new arts building features eye- catching contemporary works.

MORE INFORMATION

Flag Ponds Nature Park
>www.calvertparks.org/fpp.html
>1525 Flag Ponds Parkway, Lusby
>410-586-1477
>Open Memorial Day-Labor Day
>>Monday-Friday, 9am-6pm
>>Saturday-Sunday, 9am-8pm
>>Rest of year Friday-Sunday, 9am-4pm
>Entrance fee April-October, $5 for in-county
>>residents, $15 for non-residents
>Plan ahead for capacity closures

Calvert Marine Museum
>www.calvertmarinemuseum.com
>14200 Solomons Island Road, Solomons
>410-326-2042
>Open daily, 10:15am-4:45pm
>Entrance fee $11/adult, $9/senior
>1 hour Wm. B Tennison boat cruise May-October,
>>Wednesday-Sunday, 2pm, $7/adult

Annmarie Sculpture Garden and Arts Center
>www.annmariegarden.org
>13470 Dowell Road, Solomons
>410-326-4640
>Sculpture Garden open Monday-Friday, 9am-5pm
>>Saturday-Sunday, 10am-5pm
>>Arts Building daily, 10am-5pm
>Suggested donation $5/person

Trip 23 – Discovering New and Improved Leonardtown

WHY: If you haven't been to St. Mary's County seat recently, you'll be surprised. It's had a facelift—a brand new waterfront with a special kayak-launching pad, some new upscale restaurants, and a winery from vineyards that have replaced tobacco fields.

WHERE: From the Capital Beltway in Maryland, take SR5 (Exit 7A) south toward Waldorf. SR5 turns left after 12 miles at a traffic light and then left again after three more miles as it becomes Leonardtown Road. Just after crossing into St. Mary's County, stop at the Welcome Center in Charlotte Hall to get some travel literature and to get briefed on the many tourist attractions in the county. Leonardtown is only 11 miles down the road from that point, clearly marked. As you drive into town, turn right on SR245 to the city center. The town sights and the restaurant are on the left, and the Wharf is at the end of the road. If you drive to the winery after visiting the town, turn left on SR5 and take the first road to the left before the shopping center (Newtowne Neck Road). There is a sign to the winery. Get back on SR5 after your visit and follow it back to the Beltway.

HOW LONG: From the Beltway, it is 45 miles to Leonardtown and takes a little over an hour, not counting the stop at the Visitor Center. The sights in town take only an hour to see. After looking around the waterfront, we ate lunch. The afternoon kayak trip along McIntosh Run, a five-mile round trip, takes about two hours but can take longer if you stop to observe the birdlife. The winery has a small tasting room.

LUNCH BREAK: The **Front Porch Restaurant** (22770 Washington Street) is in an historic two-story house (built 1850) subdivided into large comfortable rooms. There is also seating on the front porch in good weather, hence its name. The menu is large and varied, with a local favorite in season—fried okra.

HIGHLIGHTS: **Leonardtown**'s historic highlights include the quaint **Old Jail Museum** and Visitor Center, and **Tudor Hall**, built on a land parcel granted in the 1640s. The latter is interesting architecturally outside and genealogically inside because it houses the historical society and local archives. The town was named after Maryland's first governor, Leonard Calvert, and was settled in 1654.

The newly completed **Wharf** puts a proper focus on the town's gorgeous water view at the confluence of Breton Bay and McIntosh Run. The 58-acre bird sanctuary along the Run is inhabited by blue heron, bald eagles (we saw two pairs with their

juveniles), orioles, and other wildlife. Interpretive markers along the water promenade explain the flora and fauna as well as the economic importance of the place in bygone times: it was a busy steamboat landing that handled tobacco and other farm products, including bootleg whiskey during prohibition. A two and a half-mile kayak/canoe trail from the Wharf into the Run (hew to the right side) terminates at a crude wharf next to the **Port of Leonardtown Winery**. This relatively new endeavor combines the grapes of three counties' growers in a co-op that also manages and guides the winery. Its repertoire includes a Chardonnay, Vidal Blanc, a semi- sweet apple wine, and a dessert wine. As you drive along St. Mary's roads, be sure not to miss the buggy lanes reserved for the Amish and the many weathered tobacco barns, which are now museum pieces.

MORE INFORMATION

Historic Leonardtown
> www.leonardtown.somd.com
> 301-475-9791
> Town's website has a virtual tour with street and
> aerial views.

Old Jail Museum and Visitor Center
> www.visitstmarysmd.com/activities-attractions/
> 41625 Courthouse Drive, Leonardtown
> 240-925-3427
> Open daily, 10am-5pm

Tudor Hall
> www.visitstmarysmd.com/activities-attractions/
> 41680 Tudor Place, Leonardtown
> 301-475-2467
> Open Thursday-Friday, 11am-4pm

Port of Leonardtown Winery
> www.polwinery.com
> 23190 Newtowne Neck Road, Leonardtown
> 301-690-2192
> Tasting room hours Sunday-Friday,12pm-6pm
> Saturday, 12pm-8pm

**Patuxent Adventure Center - Leonardtown Wharf and
Port of Leonardtown** (for kayak and paddleboard rental)
> www.pacpaddle.com
> 410-394-2770

Trip 24 – The Lower Patuxent: from Hogsheads to Contrails

WHY: St. Mary's County is a place of old and new along the Patuxent shoreline. Visit Patuxent Naval Air Station, the country's center for testing of the Navy's experimental aircraft and then bike to Maryland's only tidewater plantation, Sotterley.

WHERE: From the Capital Beltway in Maryland, take SR5 (Exit 7A) south toward Waldorf. After 32 miles, go straight ahead on SR235 toward Lexington Park. In 17 miles, you will see the Naval Air Museum on your left. After your visit, drive a couple of miles southeast to the lunch spot and then drive back to the Hollywood Volunteer Fire Department, which will be on your left. Bike from their large public parking lot. First bike north one- fifth of a mile on SR235, turning right at Old Three Notch Road and then left on Vista Road. You will reach Sotterley in about four and a half miles. After the tour, follow the Exit sign, turn left on SR245, and then left on Steer Horn Neck Road. Follow this road in a loop along the Patuxent and then back to SR245 where you turn left. This road returns you to SR235. Turn right, back to the Fire Department. Retrace your drive back along SR235 and SR5 to the Beltway.

HOW LONG: It takes a little more than an hour to reach the Patuxent Naval Air Museum, where you can easily spend an hour. After lunch, the bike ride to Sotterley takes 30 minutes. The tour is about 45 minutes but leave extra time for a short walk to the slave cabin and the gardens. The rest of the bike tour takes one and a half hours, and the drive back to the Beltway is less than an hour.

LUNCH BREAK: Pax River Ale House (46590 Corporate Dr.) has classic pub fare and 30+beers on tap.

HIGHLIGHTS: **Patuxent River Naval Air Museum** focuses on the history of the last 70 years of naval aviation testing. Outside are 25 aircraft and inside are exhibits of such things as test instruments, jet engines and crew ejection seats. On weekends you can try out a flight simulator ($10 for a half hour). Some of the more interesting exhibits are the prototypes that never went into production such as the UAV designed to drop torpedoes on submarines. Something to ponder is the courage—or insanity—that inspired the first navy airmen who volunteered to test ejection seats.

Sotterley Plantation now covers 100 acres, but it once encompassed 7,000. Its plantation house was originally built in 1703 as a modest two-room farmhouse, but after many owners and additions it was large enough to hold a family with 13 children. One of its owners became the 6th governor of Maryland. It fell into disrepair over the years and was saved and lovingly restored in the early 1900s by a gentleman from New York named Satterlee who could trace his roots back to the same family in England. The house is a poor cousin of the grandiose plantation homes of Virginia, but it commands a lovely view of the Patuxent and has a beautiful colonial-inspired garden. It is easy to imagine the enslaved rolling huge hogsheads of tobacco down the winding lane to the wharf where ships awaited the precious cargo.

The Sotterley Slave Cabin is one of only a few structures still standing in St. Mary's County that sheltered well over half of southern Maryland's antebellum residents. It measures 16 by 18 feet with a loft above and a floor of hard-packed dirt or clay with a root cellar in front of the fireplace. A total of 17,506 artifacts were recovered from the site including oyster shell fragments, building materials and animal bones.

MORE INFORMATION

Patuxent River Naval Air Museum
    www.paxmuseum.com
    22156 Three Notch Road, Lexington Park
    301-863-1900
    Open Tuesday-Saturday, 10am-5pm
        Sunday, noon-5pm
    Entrance fee $10/adults, $7/active duty and seniors

Sotterley Plantation
    www.sotterley.org
    44300 Sotterley Lane, Hollywood
    301-373-2280
    Open year-round except major holidays
        Monday-Saturday, 10am-4pm
        Sunday, 11:30am-4 pm
    Mansion guided tours Thursday-Saturday, 10:30am,
        11:30am, 1pm, 2pm, and 3pm
        Sunday tours noon, 1pm, 2pm, and 3pm
    Entrance fee for guided tour $10/adult, $9/senior
    Entrance fee for self-guided tours $5/person

Trip 25 – Tour Maryland's Birthplace and then Bike to a Sad Remnant of the Civil War

WHY: Historic St. Mary's City, by a fluke of history, is one of America's best preserved archaeological sites. Down the road by bike or car is strategically located Point Lookout, the site of a horrific prisoner of war camp during the Civil War. Built to hold 10,000 Confederate prisoners, it eventually held 50,000, with predictable results.

WHERE: From the Capital Beltway in Maryland, take SR5 (Exit 7A) south. Historic St. Mary's City is 60 miles away. After a morning there, continue on SR5 south for six miles and turn right at Ridge onto Wynne Road. Take it to the end to reach the lunch stop. Come back to Ridge and park at Ridge Market if you want to bike to Point Lookout. The route is well marked to all of the sights.

HOW LONG: It takes a little less than one and a half hours to reach Historic St. Mary's City. A visit to both sites (the main one and St. John's Museum on the campus of St. Mary's College) takes the whole morning and then some. The lunch spot is only six miles away. The round-trip bike ride to Point Lookout is 13 miles beyond the lunch spot and flat, but if you take all the possible side trips, it could take two hours or more. The trip home traces the same route in reverse—north on SR5 to the Beltway—so is about one and a half hours.

LUNCH BREAK: **Courtney's Restaurant and Seafood** (48290 Wynne Road in Ridge) is located on a picturesque inlet of the Potomac River. It is the essence of Southern Maryland cooking—plain but fresh.

HIGHLIGHTS: **Historic St. Mary's City** is the site of Maryland's first colony and capital, established by English settlers in

1634, not long after the founding of Jamestown and Plymouth. The capital was moved to Annapolis in 1695, and St. Mary's went into an abrupt decline, the buildings cannibalized for other sites and the land turned under plow. This did a remarkable job of preserving history almost intact. Start at the Visitor Center to see the 10-minute orientation video because you need to use your time wisely; there is a lot to see. Walk the trails through the old city and you'll find some sites reconstructed, such as the handsome State House and the Catholic Church, while others are called ghost frames because they stand where buildings once were. Period-costumed guides give you insights into life back then. Take the path to the river and see the recreation of the *Maryland Dove*, the vessel that carried the first settlers here. Don't miss the superb **St. John's Site Museum**

(costing the state $10 million) located off College Drive in the heart of the St. Mary's campus. It uses the latest technology and museum science to give you the feeling that you are stepping back into events that shaped Maryland and the nation.

Point Lookout State Park, on the peninsula where the Potomac and Chesapeake meet, is now a peaceful destination for boaters, hikers and campers—in sharp contrast to its function during the Civil War as a hospital for Union soldiers and then a prison for captured Confederate soldiers. Living in miserable conditions, almost 4,000 prisoners died. Park headquarters has a small museum that tells this story, and there are also several monuments along the road to those who died. Go further south across the causeway and you'll find the picturesque old lighthouse, built in 1830 but no longer operational.

MORE INFORMATION

Historic St. Mary's City
  hsmcdigshistory.org
  18751 Hogaboom Lane, St. Mary's City
  240-895-4990
  Open March 14-July 1, Tuesday-Saturday, 10am-4pm
      July 5-September 3, Wednesday-Sunday, 10am-4pm
      Sept 5-November 25, Tuesday-Saturday, 10am-4pm
  Listen to the audio tour on your smart phone
  Entrance fee $10/adult, $9/senior

St. John's Site Museum
  hsmcdigshistory/org/map/St. John's Site
  College Drive (off SR5 on St. Mary's College
      Campus)
  1-800-SMC-1634
  Same hours as Historic St. Mary's City
  Entrance free but suggested donation $5

Point Lookout State Park
  dnr.maryland.gov/publiclands/Pages/southern/
      pointlookout.aspx
  1175 Point Lookout Road, Scotland
  301-872-5688
  Open May-September, 7am-sunset
      Civil War Museum open May-October
  Entrance fees May to September
      Weekends, MD residents $5, out-of-state $7
      Weekdays, MD residents $3, out-of-state $5

Trip 26 – London Town (Maryland's Own) by Water

WHY: Launching a kayak from one of the prettiest county parks in the state allows you to paddle to a great seafood restaurant and then visit the remnants of one of colonial Maryland's earliest towns.

WHERE: From the Capital Beltway, take Exit 19A onto John Hanson Highway (US50). In about 20 miles, take Exit 22, Aris T. Allen Blvd. (SR665). Merge onto Forest Drive and in three miles, turn right at Hillsmere Drive. Immediately turn right into Quiet Waters Park. Follow the signs to the boat launch and rental shop. Once on the water, Harness Creek, paddle left and then right onto South River. In about three miles you will come to a large bridge carrying Solomons Island Road over the water. Turn right past the bridge and pull up at the marina onto a small sandy beach. The lunch spot is next to the marina. After lunch, return along the right bank of South River about a mile and past a large housing development and you will see the Brown House (a large 17th century brick house) at London Town. Leave your boat at their pier or along the shore. After your visit, return along the same route to Quiet Waters Park and then drive home.

HOW LONG: From the Beltway it takes about 30 minutes to get to Quiet Waters Park. It can take one and a half hours to paddle to the lunch spot if the water is choppy. After lunch, it's an hour's paddle back to London Town. On a pleasant day you can spend an hour visiting London Town and then it's another hour back to Quiet Waters.

LUNCH BREAK: **Yellowfin Steak and Fish House** (2840 Solomons Island Road) at Edgewater is a surprise—somewhat plain on the outside but inside an extensive and imaginative menu, including a sushi platter.

HIGHLIGHTS: Anne Arundel County's **Quiet Waters Park** is a beautifully landscaped and maintained park with over six miles of trails, boat rentals (canoe, kayak, and paddle boats), bicycle rentals, and even an ice-skating rink. Paddling Harness Creek and South River displays an architectural delight of homes. You can also see osprey nests.

London Town and Gardens is a 23-acre historic site that encompasses the remains of a colonial tobacco port founded in 1683 and a grand old brick mansion, the William Brown House, built in the early 1760s. Ships arrived here each fall to take the locally grown tobacco to Britain for sale. It was also the site of an important ferry that saved about 20 miles of travel by road. The town declined with the tobacco trade and then a rival ferry upriver diverted travelers from the town. The Brown House remained a ghost of the town until it became the county almshouse in the 1820s. It was restored to its original condition in 1965 and furnished with period pieces. The old port buildings are being reconstructed including the carpenter shop and colonial kitchen, and days are set aside for the public to dig with professional archaeologists. An eight-acre Woodland Garden arranged along a one-mile trail features a botanical collection of native plants and exotic species.

MORE INFORMATION

Quiet Waters Park

    www.aacounty.org/RecParks/parks/quietwaters/
        index.html

    600 Quiet Waters Park Road, Annapolis

    410-222-1777

    Open daily, dawn-dusk

    Entrance fee $6/vehicle

    Single kayak rental $15/hour or $45/day
        Bicycle rental $10/hour or $30/day

Historic London Town and Gardens

    www.historiclondontown.org

    839 Londontown Road, Edgewater

    410-222-1919

    Open Wednesday-Sunday, 10am-4pm
        30-minute outside walking tours at 11am and
        2:30pm

    Entrance fee $11/adult, $10/senior 62+

Trip 27 – Paddling to Maryland's Water-luvin' Capital

WHY: Annapolis is a treat no matter the conveyance chosen, but getting there by boat takes you back to an era when the water was the main highway. Take the opportunity while there to visit a museum that profiles African Americans who led the fight for equality; you'll be surprised how many were born in Maryland.

WHERE: From the Capital Beltway, take Exit 19A onto John Hanson Highway (US50). In about 20 miles, take Exit 22, Aris T. Allen Blvd./Forest Drive (SR665) for about four miles. Turn left at Hilltop Lane and after about one mile, turn left on Primrose Road. Stay left at the fork and continue on Park Road to Truxtun Park. Paddle to the left and then around the corner to the right on Spa Creek. You'll soon come to a bridge (from Annapolis to Eastport), and the **Annapolis City Dock** is down the branch immediately to the left. If you want to paddle a little longer before lunch, go along the sea wall by the Naval Academy on the Severn River and turn left into College Creek where you'll find St. John's College. After returning to the City Dock and having lunch, walk up the hill on Main Street and follow the traffic circle around to Franklin Street. Turn left and the museum is on the left. Return home along the same route that you came.

HOW LONG: From the Beltway it takes about 30 minutes to get to Truxtun Park. A paddle straight to the City Dock is only one and a half miles but can take an hour or longer if you meander. The lunch spot is within sight of the Dock. The museum is only one-quarter of a mile from the restaurant; your visit there will take less than an hour because it is very small.

LUNCH BREAK: **Buddy's Crabs and Ribs** (100 Main Street) has an all-you-can-eat lunch, but the best seafood is on the a la carte menu. The crabcake and soft shell crab sandwiches are juicy and plump, and the fries are excellent.

HIGHLIGHTS: Anne Arundel County's **Truxtun Park** has a wonderful launch area (free for kayaks) on Spa Creek that is your ticket to a fascinating shoreline of beautiful homes and boats on your way to Annapolis. You won't see much wildlife other than ducks and seagulls, but you'll see interesting varieties of homo sapiens, who are all enjoying the "land of pleasant living." It is fun to paddle into the City Dock past monstrous yachts and riverside tables, but it is somewhat uncomfortable, under the gaze of many tourists, to alight gracefully from your kayak to a ladder that allows you access to dry  land. The area around the dock is filled with restaurants, art galleries, and touristy shops.

The **Banneker-Douglass Museum** is named for Benjamin Banneker, the Maryland-born mathematician who helped survey and lay out the District of Columbia, and Frederick Douglass, who escaped slavery to become a leader of the abolition movement. The Mt. Moriah African Methodist Episcopal Church built in 1874 that originally housed the museum—now in a handsome new facility next door— was the first black institution in the city to be preserved for its historic value. The museum, with its well-displayed contents, tells the history of slavery and the fight for civil rights through interesting profiles of black leaders. Interactive exhibits allow you to listen to music and the words of these leaders as well as to step back in time to the civil rights marches in Cambridge that led to the town being occupied by the Maryland National Guard in 1963.

MORE INFORMATION

Truxtun Park at Spa Creek
    www.annapolis.gov/173/Boat-Ramps
    273 Hilltop Lane, Annapolis
    410-263-7958
    Open daily, 6am-9pm
    Entrance free

Annapolis Canoe and Kayak
    annapoliscanoeandkayak.com
    311 3rd Street, Annapolis (Eastport)
    410-263-2303
    Single kayaks rent for $20/hour or $50/day

Banneker-Douglass Museum
    bdmuseum.maryland.gov
    84 Franklin Street, Annapolis
    410-216-6180
    Open Tuesday-Saturday, 10am-4pm
    Entrance free, donations encouraged
    Virtual tour of the museum on its website

Trip 28 – Biking on the Flat across Kent Island

WHY: Have you only thought of Kent Island as a place to pass through quickly on the way to Ocean City? Well, that's a pity because it holds many delights—as a multi-sport destination (biking, hiking, kayaking, and rollerblading) and as a seafood smorgasbord.

WHERE: From the Capital Beltway, take US50 east to Exit 37 (just after crossing the Chesapeake Bay Bridge), and turn left on SR8. Turn left at the second light into Chesapeake Bay Business Park and follow the road to the right around the circle until you come to Terrapin Nature Park on your right. The trail head at the parking lot is clearly marked. Take the trail to the end, and then continue the ride by going under the large bridge (SR50) and over the old drawbridge (SR18) until you come to a roundabout with a sculpture of watermen. Continue on SR18 for two miles, turning right onto Perry's Corner Road. The entrance to Chesapeake Bay Environmental Center is about one half of a mile on the right. Follow Discovery Lane to the Visitor Center. On your way back, stop at Kent Narrows for lunch.

HOW LONG: From the Capital Beltway, it is 32.4 miles to the trailhead at Terrapin Nature Park, which takes about 40 minutes. The bike route from there to the Chesapeake Bay Environmental Center and back is about 20 miles, and the biking time is around two hours as it is all on the flat. Add time for wandering around the Environmental Center's large property and a possible short detour on the way back (clearly marked) to the Chesapeake Heritage and Visitor Center and, of course, lunch.

LUNCH BREAK: Seafood restaurants abound in Kent Narrows after you go across the bridge. We ate at **Harris Crab House**'s top deck (433 Kent Narrow Way) —a great view and great crab.

HIGHLIGHTS: **The Cross Island Trail** spans Kent Island in Queen Anne's County and is a five and a half-mile gem. It winds along boardwalks and smooth asphalt, through pine and hardwood forest that almost always shades the path, and is virtually flat, making it a popular spot for rollerblading. You pass over marshes with heron and egret, see a red lighthouse in the distance, go through a community park, and come too soon to the trail's terminus at Kent Narrows. If you've gotten a late start, you can eat lunch here and then head to the sights.

Chesapeake Bay Environmental Center. This parcel of 510 acres of pristine wetlands was preserved in 1979 by the Wildfowl Trust of North America as a direct response to the dwindling waterfowl population of the Chesapeake Bay. It has four miles of land trails, canoe, and kayak trails, two observation towers, two concealed observation blinds, and marsh boardwalks that provide visitor-access to this watery ecosystem. Near the Visitor Center, you can see a collection of non- releasable raptors, demonstration gardens, backyard habitats, and a constructed wetland to try in your own backyard. If you join the Wildfowl Trust (individual membership $35), you can enjoy these wonders for free. On the way back, just before you pick up the Cross Island Trail, follow the signs to the **Chesapeake Heritage and Visitor Center**, the county's Visitor Center. It has a deluge of information on local things to do as well as a small museum on the history of

the land where crabs were once thought of as a nuisance. The Center has a high observation deck, and a 530-foot boardwalk over marsh and field is part of the adjacent **Ferry Point Park**.

MORE INFORMATION

Cross Island Trail
> www.traillink.com/trail/cross-island-trail/
> 410-758-0835
> Open daily, dawn-dusk
> Entrance free

Chesapeake Bay Environmental Center
> www.bayrestoration.org
> 600 Discovery Lane, Grasonville
> 410-827-6694
> Open daily, 9am-5pm
> Kayak rental $20/day
> Memberships or donations are encouraged

Chesapeake Heritage and Visitor Center
> qac.org
> 425 Piney Narrows Road, Chester
> 410-604-2100
> Open daily, 10am-4pm
> Ferry Point Park open dawn-dusk
> Entrance free

Trip 29 – Enjoying Kent County by Foot and by Paddle

WHY: As the president of the National Trust for Historic Preservation said, "Chestertown is a treasure hidden in plain sight." It is an unspoiled town on the Eastern Shore that is largely bypassed by the hordes heading toward the Atlantic beaches. In nearby Gratitude and Rock Hall, kayaking in quiet coves away from power boats allows you to observe osprey and cormorants.

WHERE: From the Capital Beltway, take US50 east over the Bay Bridge to SR301 north. Exit at SR213 toward Chestertown. In Chestertown, turn left at Cross Street and stop at the Kent County Visitor Center for a walking tour map. After a walk and lunch, drive west on Cross Street and then right on High Street, which is SR20, and go about 15 miles to the little town of Gratitude. On the right is Osprey Point Marina where you can put in your kayak at their tiny beach or rent one on Main St. After boating, stop for ice cream in Rock Hall at **Durding's Store** (corner of Main and Sharp Streets) and then retrace your steps through Chestertown and home.

HOW LONG: This trip reaches the limit of our day trips—a total of one hour 25 minutes from the Capital Beltway turnoff on SR50 to the end point, the town of Gratitude. The Beltway turnoff to Chestertown is one hour 10 minutes. The walking tour of Chestertown can take an hour, and two hours makes for a nice paddle out of Gratitude.

LUNCH BREAK: Not far from the Visitor Center is **Fig's Ordinary** (207 S. Cross St.). A gluten-free and vegan restaurant, it gets good reviews for food and service.

HIGHLIGHTS: **Chestertown** on the Chester River has served as Kent County's seat of government since 1706. Its prominence was ensured when it was named one of the English colonies of Maryland's six Royal Ports of Entry. The ensuing shipping boom made the town wealthy and the prosperous merchant class built brick mansions and townhouses close to the waterfront. It is second only to Annapolis in its number of eighteenth-century homes still extant. Because of their size and concentration along what was the wharf area, they are more impressive than those in Annapolis. Styles range from Georgian, built in the Revolutionary era, to Italianate, built in the mid-eighteenth century. Twenty four sites are on the walking tour. In May 1774, five months after the Boston Tea Party, the citizens of Chestertown held their own tea party on the Chester River in an act of colonial defiance. The Chestertown Tea Party Festival every year in May celebrates this event. Re-enactors playing the part of angry citizens and Continental soldiers march to the dock where they skirmish and board a reproduction of the British Navy ship, the schooner Sultana. Chestertown is also the home of Washington College, a private liberal arts college that had George Washington as a founding patron.

The towns of **Rock Hall** and **Gratitude**, on Chesapeake Bay just down the road from Chestertown, are major centers for pleasure boaters and charter boats that allow you to catch your own dinner. A wealth of charming B&Bs and seafood restaurants vie for the visitor's attention. Because most of the commercial boats head for Chesapeake Bay, the little coves are the private preserve of kayaks and canoes.

MORE INFORMATION

Kent County Visitors Center
townofchestertown.com/visitors
122 North Cross Street, Chestertown
410-778-9737
Open year-round, daily, Monday-Friday, 9am-5pm
Weekends in winter, 10am-2pm
Weekends in summer, 10am-4pm

Kayak Rental – Chester River Kayak Adventures:
www.crkayakadventures.com
5758 Main Street, Rock Hall
410-639-2001

Trip 30 – A Day in the City: A Tour of Two Museums Contrasting the New and Old Worlds

WHY: These two museums in Washington were chosen because they are off the beaten tourist track and have lovely gardens in wooded settings that belie their in-town locations.

WHERE: Both museums are easy to find from all compass points. Hillwood overlooks Rock Creek Park, and Dumbarton Oaks sits high above Georgetown. From the Capital Beltway in Maryland, take Connecticut Avenue Exit south. In about five miles, turn left onto Tilden Street. Take the second left onto Linnean Avenue. The entrance to the estate is on the right. When you leave Hillwood, go west on Tilden, right on Reno Road, left on Van Ness Street and then left on Wisconsin, which you follow down to R Street. Turn left on R Street and then right on 32nd Street, and the museum is at 1703 32nd Street, right before S Street. Go to Hillwood first.

HOW LONG: Opening at 10am, you can tour Hillwood indoors before lunch, tour the grounds after lunch, and then leave for Dumbarton Oaks, which closes at 5:30pm.

LUNCH BREAK: The **Merriweather Cafe** at Hillwood is open from 11am to 3:30pm. Enjoy a tasty lunch (sandwiches and borscht).

HIGHLIGHTS: **Hillwood Estate, Museum and Gardens**, "where fabulous lives" (as the advertisement goes), was the home of Marjorie Merriweather Post in her later years and was remodeled to be the repository for her large collection of French decorative art and Russian imperial art. As the only heir of C.W. Post of cereal fame, she had the means and desire to fill her homes with French pieces early in her married life but began her interest

88

in Russian art after living in Moscow from 1937-38 with her third husband, the US Ambassador. Her most famous collection is the incredible Faberge eggs given as gifts among the Russian imperial family every Easter. You can download the mansion audio tour (please bring headphones).

Beginning in April, 13 acres of gardens reveal their beauty and include a French parterre, Japanese-style garden, a rose garden, and numerous other "garden rooms." Special tours focus on different parts of the garden (see website for times and fees).

Dumbarton Oaks Research Library and Collection is an institute of Harvard University and contains a world-class collection of Byzantine and pre-Columbian art. The house and the art were bequeathed by William Bliss, a Foreign Service officer and diplomat, who was the US Ambassador to Argentina during 1927-33. The pre-Columbian pieces are exquisitely displayed in glass cases like the gems that they are. Docents unobtrusively offer additional information to visitors. Heavily endowed, Dumbarton Oaks' main priority is its visiting scholar program. It welcomes scholars to consult its books, images, and objects, and the public to visit its exquisite gardens, museum, and music room for lectures and concerts.

MORE INFORMATION

Hillwood

> www.hillwoodmuseum.org
> 4155 Linnean Avenue, Washington DC
> 202-686-5807
> Open Tuesday-Saturday, 10am-5pm
> Entrance fee $18/adult, $15/senior (includes audio
> tour)

Dumbarton Oaks

> www.doaks.org
> 1703 32nd Street, Washington DC (2-hour street
> parking is available)
> 202-339-6400
> Open daily except Monday, 11:30am-5:30pm
> Gardens open daily except Monday, 2pm-6pm
> March 15- October 31
> Entrance free to museum but $7/adult for the
> gardens in season (docent-led tours available)

Trip 31 – Looking at Both Sides of the Potomac

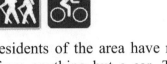

WHY: Even long-time residents of the area have not seen this stretch of the Potomac from anything but a car. The Potomac Heritage Trail hugs the river below the bluffs that edge the GW Parkway, and the return bike trip along the C&O canal comes full circle.

WHERE: The best way to juggle the bikes is to take them first via the George Washington Parkway to the bike rack at Teddy Roosevelt Island. Coming from the North, take the turnoff to Memorial Bridge beyond Teddy Roosevelt Bridge so that you can return to the GW Parkway going north and pull off into the T.R. Island parking lot. Hitch your bikes to the rack and drive north about five miles, leaving the GW Parkway at SR123, turning north toward DC. Turn right at the stoplight on Glebe Road and park in the small parking lot to the right. The beginning of the trail is directly across from the parking lot and goes under Chain Bridge. After retrieving your bikes at the end of the hike, go across Key Bridge and turn right before M Street on a path down to the canal. Stay on the canal tow path (do not get on the Crescent Trail) and cross back to Virginia via Chain Bridge.

HOW LONG: It takes less than half of an hour to reach the T.R. Island parking lot from I-495 and the same to get your car back to the beginning of the Potomac Heritage Trail. The three and three quarter-mile hike along the trail back to the bikes takes about two and a half hours. After lunch, the bike ride back along the towpath is less than an hour. *Warning*: This hiking trail is one of the most challenging in this book. Although well marked, the first part bears only a faint resemblance to a trail and requires hazardous climbs over rock formations that reach down into the river and the fording of streams. Go only in dry weather. The last part of the route is easy walking along a well-worn path.

LUNCH BREAK: You have your pick of restaurants in Rosslyn (go across a little bridge at the end of the parking lot to get there). We ate at **Cosi** (1801 N. Lynne Street, the road across Key Bridge). A light sandwich and a smoothie were perfect after the strenuous morning.

HIGHLIGHTS: **Potomac Heritage National Scenic Trail** is an evolving 830-mile network of locally managed trails and routes that embraces both sides of the Potomac River. The four-mile route hiked between Chain Bridge and Key Bridge is a secluded segment (we did not see any other hikers), probably because of its primitive nature and difficulty. At mid-point you see only some fisherman on the opposite shore, flocks of cormorants also fishing, and an occasional rowboat or kayak. Hiked in spring, there are groves of bluebells and surprisingly high waterfalls falling off the bluffs. Download "Potomac Heritage Trail Map."

After the hike, cross the small bridge and visit **Teddy Roosevelt Island National Memorial**, a tribute to our 26th President, who was an avid outdoorsman and conservationist. On the DC side of the river, the Georgetown Visitor Center of the **C&O Canal National Historical Park** is finally open after years of closure and a Canal boat ride is available in Georgetown. Georgetown is the terminus of the 184.5 miles of the park. The C&O Canal was once a lifeline for communities and businesses along the Potomac River as coal, lumber, grain, and other farm products floated down the canal to market.

MORE INFORMATION

Potomac Heritage National Scenic Trail
     www.nps.gov/pohe/index.htm
     304-535-4014

Teddy Roosevelt Island National Memorial
     www.nps.gov/this/index.htm
     Open year-round, daily, 6am-10pm
     Download the simple trail map and a handy bird
         checklist

C&O Canal National Historical Park at mile 0.4 on the
towpath
     Open Wednesday-Sunday, 9:30am-5pm
     For canal boat rides see georgetownheritage.org

Trip 32 – Enjoying President Lincoln's Cottage and the Recovering Anacostia River

WHY: Few Washington area residents know about these two spots: the first because only history buffs remember where President Lincoln and his family sheltered during the Civil War and the second because for centuries the river was too polluted to enjoy.

WHERE: Start the day by following your travel app to Lincoln's Cottage at 140 Rock Creek Church Road (just east of the Petworth neighborhood in DC) and then eat lunch nearby on your way to Kenilworth Aquatic Gardens, where you'll park for your bike ride. Your travel app can tell you about the best route between the two points depending on the time of day.

HOW LONG: Spend the morning at Lincoln's Cottage, eat lunch and devote the afternoon to biking along the river. After reading the TrailLink description of the 12-mile Anacostia River Trail, you can decide which direction and how far appeals to you starting from Kenilworth Gardens—toward the Bladensburg Waterfront Park or the other way towards Nationals Park, or maybe both.

LUNCH BREAK: Near Catholic University, on the way to Kenilworth Gardens from Lincoln's Cottage, is **Bus Boys and Poets**, self-described as a "hip hangout for books, bites and coffee" (625 Monroe St. NE). The menu is large and diverse, including a quinoa bowl, fried catfish, and a Mediterranean lamb burger.

HIGHLIGHTS: President Lincoln's Cottage is a national monument on the grounds of the Soldiers' Home, which is located on a picturesque hilltop in Northwest DC. The home served as an escape from the heat and the political pressures for many Presidents (Buchanan, Hayes, and Arthur) but it is best known for Lincoln's residency during the Civil War. There he drafted the Emancipation Proclamation. The adjacent Robert H. Smith Visitor Education Center features exhibits about the Soldier's Home, wartime Washington D.C., and Lincoln as Commander-in-Chief during the Civil War. Take a guided tour of the house or, with a self-guided app, you can tour the grounds—9 stops on a 1-1/2 mile route.

Anacostia Riverwalk Trail is a 12-mile route from Nationals Park at S. Capitol and O Streets to the Bladensburg Waterfront Park. Heavy pollution, mainly the emptying of raw sewage, and weak investment along its banks once made it "D.C.'s forgotten river." More recently, private organizations, local businesses and the adjoining governments have helped reduce its pollution and protect this ecologically valuable watershed. The Riverwalk is an ongoing project that will eventually connect with other trails that will take you to the National Arboretum and the Maine Avenue Fish market. **Kenilworth Park and Aquatic Gardens**, now on its route, is a National Park Service gem that preserves a plethora of rare waterlilies and lotuses in cultivated ponds near the river. The Audubon Society has  spotted 59 species of birds there in different seasons.

MORE INFORMATION

President Lincoln's Cottage
> www.lincolncottage.org
> 140 Rock Creek Church Rd.
> 202-829-0436
> Open daily, 9:30am-4:30pm
> Guided tours on the hour; buy tickets in advance;
> > Valid ID at the security gate required to enter
> Cottage tour fee $15/adult

Anacostia Riverwalk Trail
> www.traillink.com/trail/anacostia-river-trail/
> > (Download Trail Map by Rails-to-Trails
> > Conservancy)

Kenilworth Park and Aquatic Gardens
> www.nps.gov>keaq
> 1550 Anacostia Ave. NE Washington, DC
> Open 362 days a year
> Entrance free

Trip 33 – Hiking along the Virginia Side of the Great Falls of the Potomac

WHY: Enjoy the best views of the most impressive natural wonder in Northern Virginia.

WHERE: Scott's Run Nature Preserve in McLean is less than one mile from the Capital Beltway on Georgetown Pike (SR193) going toward Great Falls. Go six miles further along Georgetown Pike and you'll come to a right turn-off to Great Falls Park. Follow the park road. If you want to go first into the town of Great Falls to stock up for lunch, continue on Georgetown Pike beyond the turnoff to the park and you'll come to the town's center in one and a half miles.

HOW LONG: About five miles of leisurely hiking takes about three and a half hours. Some of the terrain is difficult—rocky and uneven.

LUNCH BREAK: There are no restaurants between the two parks. Pick up some deli sandwiches made fresh at Great Falls **Safeway** (9881 Georgetown Pike) or go to **Subway** in the same shopping center and consume them on the trail.

HIGHLIGHTS: **Scott's Run Nature Preserve**: This tract was saved from suburban development by Fairfax County in the 1970s and remains a quiet green zone between busy Georgetown Pike and the Potomac. It has only a few remnants of human habitation, including a grand old fireplace of the ruined Burling House. Start in the second parking lot on the right from the Beltway and follow the trail at the end of the parking lot along Scott's Run (warning: this is a very busy parking lot on the weekends). When you come to a set of stairs in the woods, don't take them yet but go down to the river; there is a very pretty little waterfall cascading into the Potomac surrounded by blue wildflowers in the spring. Then retrace your steps and go up the staircase and follow the well-marked circular route through the woods back to the parking lot. You can't get lost. The Potomac is on the north and Georgetown Pike is on the south. You'll see few people but a good variety of flora and fauna. The trail is about two miles in length.

Great Falls Park is not only the premier natural wonder in the area but also a historic site, the ruins of a grand series of canals aimed at fulfilling George Washington's dream—making the river navigable. Start by looking out from all three overlooks closest to the Visitor Center. Also note the flood markers by year—hard to imagine. Now get on the River Trail, clearly marked. This trail hangs on the precipice of the breathtaking Mather Gorge, named for the first Director of the National Park Service. If you go in the spring, when the Potomac is swollen with April showers, you won't believe how the tumbling waters have erased many of the familiar rocks and even engulfed large tree trunks that are usually high above the water. Also in spring, the trails are covered with wildflowers, and some trails are underwater, but scrambling over well-positioned rocks can get you back on course. Go all the way to Cow Hoof Rock and walk back the easy way on the road built to take the kayakers down to the river (at Sandy Landing). On the way back, you can explore what's left of the canals and locks of the Patowmack Canal and the town of Matildaville, built to house the canal workers. It flourished for nearly three decades. The entire hike is about three miles long.

MORE INFORMATION

Scott's Run Nature Preserve
www.hikingupward.com/OVH/ScottsRun
Website has a description of hike with map
Entrance free

Great Falls Park
www.nps.gov/grfa
9200 Old Dominion Drive, McLean
703-757-3101
Open daily, 7am-dark
Visitor Center open daily, 10am-4pm
Entrance fee $20/vehicle

Trip 34 – An Easy Bike Ride along the W&OD Trail to Leesburg and Back

WHY: Bike on "the skinniest park in Virginia" to the historic town of Leesburg. The Leesburg area was a major crossroads for Indian tribes, played a pivotal role in the Colonial and Civil War eras, and served as temporary haven for the US government and its archives during the War of 1812.

WHERE: Take the Dulles Toll Road from the Capital Beltway to SR28 and turn north. Turn westbound on Waxpool Road, turn right onto Pacific Boulevard, pass over the W&OD bridge and then turn left into the parking lot access road. Bike from there (Mile 23.5) to Leesburg, getting off on Harrison Street at Mile 34. Turn left on Loudoun Street and continue a few blocks to the Loudoun County Museum on the right. Have lunch at Market Station, which you passed on Harrison Street. Continue biking West on Loudoun Street. Turn right on Morven Park Road to the right turnoff into Morven Park. Retrace the same route back to your car.

HOW LONG: The drive to the bike staging area from the Capital Beltway takes just one half hour. We reached Leesburg from there by bike in about an hour. Lunch and stops at the small museum and historic house take another couple of hours before heading back.

LUNCH BREAK: You can choose from several restaurants at Market Station such as **South Street Under**, the deli below the fancy Tuscarora Mill Restaurant (203 Harrison Street).

HIGHLIGHTS: The **W&OD Railroad Regional Park** is 100 feet wide and nearly 45 miles in length and is on the roadbed of the former Washington and Old Dominion Railroad. Because the trains brought hobo-ing seeds, it is a naturalist's delight with about 450 identified wildflowers. This section of the trail passes by a huge quarry, lovely creeks, and the Two Creeks trail, which is a two-mile long hiking loop that is a challenging dirt bike trail. **Leesburg**, the county seat of Loudoun County, was created in 1758 by the Virginia Assembly to honor the influential Thomas Lee (not Robert E.). Many of the First Families of Virginia were among those to settle in the area including the Carters, Lees, and Masons. After the Civil War, as the plantations declined without enslaved labor, the horse-loving wealthy set from the north bought the land. The **Loudoun County Museum** has artifacts from these various eras and includes a notable quilt collection. It has an extensive collection of archives, photos, and objects that are accessible from your computer.

Morven Park, on 1000 acres, was home to two governors—Thomas Swann of Maryland and then Virginia's reform governor, Westmoreland Davis. The mansion evolved from a fieldstone farmhouse in 1781 to its present Greek Revival style. Overpowering all, but missing today, were several Italianate-style towers, leading one Confederate soldier to call it "Swan's Castle" [sic]. Confederate troops spent the winter of 1861-62 on the grounds where replica huts are today. While Morven Park saw little military action, it lay in the path of Union soldiers and also of General Robert E. Lee's army passing through on its way to the fateful battle of Antietam. On the grounds is an admirable collection of beautiful old carriages used between the mid-1800s and the early 1900s.

MORE INFORMATION

W&OD RR Regional Park
> www.novparks.com/parks/washington-and-old-
> dominion-railroad-regional-park
> Download map from website

Loudoun Museum
> www.loudounmuseum.org
> 16 Loudoun Street, Leesburg
> 703-777-7427
> Open Friday-Sunday, 10am-4pm
> Entrance free

Morven Park
> www.morvenpark.org
> 17195 Southern Planter Lane, Leesburg
> 571-474-2754
> Mansion tours Friday-Monday, 10am-4pm on the hour
> Carriage Museum open Sundays, 12pm-5pm
> Entrance fee $10/adult including admission to the
> Winmill Carriage Collection

Trip 35 – Bike Circle Trip around Purcellville and Waterford

WHY: Bike through lovely rolling countryside in the foothills of the Blue Ridge Mountains, with a visit to the National Historic Landmark village of Waterford and an outstanding lunch spot in Purcellville.

WHERE: Located just 50 miles from the middle of DC, Purcellville is the start and finish of the bike trip. Take the Capital Beltway to the Dulles Toll Road and then the Dulles Greenway. Take Exit 1A off the Greenway, which is SR7 west and SR15 south. Take the first Purcellville exit off SR7, which is SR287 south. Turn right at Hirst Road and then left on Hatcher Road to reach the W&OD bike trail parking lot. Directions for the bike route are in the Highlights section.

HOW LONG: The bike route, hilly at times, is 12 miles long and takes about two hours. That leaves plenty of time for lunch and some antique shopping in Purcellville.

LUNCH BREAK: Ride your bikes from the parking lot on the bike path into the center of Purcellville and eat at the **Magnolias at the Mill** restaurant (198 N. 21st Street), which has excellent brick oven flatbread (aka pizza), among other things.

HIGHLIGHTS: You start and finish the bike trip at the W&OD bike trail parking lot in Purcellville. Ride away from Purcellville on the bike trail, turning left on Hamilton Station Road and then left on SR622. In a short distance, a left turn at the Main Street hill takes you into **Waterford**. The Waterford Foundation Office is in the Corner Store at the junction of Main Street and Second Street where you can pick up an informative and free guide to the town called "Walk with Us Through Waterford, Virginia." Waterford

was founded about 1733 as a Quaker village and reached its zenith right before the Civil War period. Because the large Quaker population remained loyal to the Union and steadfastly pacifist, it endured repeated Confederate harassment. When the rebels confiscated his horses and supplies, Samuel Means, a lapsed Quaker, raised a cavalry unit to fight for the Union. His "Loudoun Rangers" were the only organized Union army unit from Virginia. After the damage from the war and flight of many residents north, the town stagnated, sleeping undisturbed until the 1930s when old Waterford families led the fight to restore it. Today, visitors experience many of the same views as residents did in the nineteenth century. A good time to visit is during the first weekend in October when the Waterford Homes Tour and Crafts Exhibit draws some 30,000 visitors. Back on the bike route, go right on Main Street and look at the old mill, built around 1830. For a different route back, take Old Wheatland Road (hard-packed gravel) to Charles Town Pike. Follow the Pike about one quarter of a mile until you turn left on Berlin Turnpike, which carries you back to the W&OD bike trail into Purcellville. This road is very busy with traffic, however, and you might want to stay on the bike trail the whole way.

Purcellville, although decidedly less picturesque than Waterford, has a colorful history dating back to 1764, befitting its location on The Great Road that reached from Alexandria to Winchester. There were several marches and chases through Purcellville during the Civil War, but the town sustained no major damage. However, a series of disastrous fires in 1900 and 1914 virtually wiped out the business district, depriving the town of much of its earliest architectural heritage. After lunch is a good time to poke around the town's many antique shops. Craft breweries abound.

MORE INFORMATION

Waterford
  www.waterfordvillage.org

Trail's End Cycling Company (for bike rental)
  www.trailsendCycling.com
  201 N. 21st Street, Purcellville
  540-338-6205

Purcellville
  www.www.purcellvilleva.gov

Trip 36 – Mansions New and Old: Biking Middleburg and Walking Oatlands

WHY: Middleburg is the center of Virginia hunt country, and the mansions outside town scream new wealth. Oatlands, on the other hand, is a product of very old wealth—built in 1805 with the money of Robert "King" Carter, a man who owned almost all of what is now Fairfax and Loudoun Counties.

WHERE: Take I-66 west off the Capital Beltway and turn west on US50. Drive to Middleburg and park near The Plains Road. You will be taking a 12 mile circular bike route on the south side of town (directions in the Highlights section). After lunch, drive back on US50 and turn left on US15. Oatlands is on your right. Return to the DC area via Leesburg on SR7.

HOW LONG: The drive to Middleburg takes about an hour, and the circular bike trip about one and a half hours. The drive to Oatlands is only 30 minutes. The house tour is 45 minutes but leave time for a self-tour of the gardens.

LUNCH BREAK: There are many lunch spots in Middleburg, both plain and fancy, but a good casual one (sandwiches and wraps) is the **Red Horse Tavern** (122 W. Washington Street), where you can watch the traffic and people pass by from the front deck.

HIGHLIGHTS: The lush green countryside and the blue-green mountains in the distance make a lovely backdrop to this ride outside of **Middleburg**. Add to this the immaculate horse farms, the intricate stone walls, the successful vineyards, and the luxurious mansions, and you have an entertaining ride as well. Head out of town on The Plains Road, which becomes Halfway Road (SR626). Turn left on Landmark (SR628), which becomes SR686 and then left on SR776 back into town. You pass several wineries (Piedmont is open for tours beginning at 11am). Middleburg was established in 1787 by Revolutionary War officer and statesman Leven Powell, who bought the land from a first cousin of George Washington. People often compare it with the beautiful English countryside. It is home to the National Sporting Library (301 W. Washington Street) with 11,000 books on field sports, and it has more than 160 historical buildings listed on the National Register of Historical Places. An equestrian mecca, it hosts numerous fox hunting and steeple-chasing events.

After lunch, head for **Oatlands**, a grand old National Trust mansion built in 1805 by George Carter, the great-grandson of colonial Virginia's renowned Robert "King" Carter. He worked on it for 40 years, changing it from brick Federal style to a stucco Greek Revival. It contains period antiques and has a gorgeous five-acre parterre and terraced garden that was hand dug by the enslaved. One of the outbuildings is a propagation greenhouse, the second oldest in the country. The house has been lived in by only two families–Carter and Eustis—but Confederate officers used several rooms for a short time as a headquarters during the Civil War. The house tour is unusually informative and interesting. The garden tour is self-guided aided by a complete listing of whatever flowers are in season.

Telling All of Our Stories

"Telling All of Our Stories" is a long-term plan to research and interpret the broader story at Oatlands, going beyond the Carter and Eustis families who owned the property. The land would have appealed to American Indians for hunting and fishing, and their artifacts have been found in the Oatlands area. During the Carter period, enslaved men, women, and children lived and labored at Oatlands.

As part of this project, a database was created to record every reference to a named enslaved person. The goal was to provide a source for locating ancestors or certain individuals and learning more about these people. The first phase consists of names extracted from George Carter's will of 1842. The database contains over 900 entries, including approximately 120 distinctly different names.

MORE INFORMATION

Middleburg
>   www.middleburgva.gov

Oatlands
>   www.oatlands.org
>   20850 Oatlands Plantation Lane, Leesburg
>   703-727-0670
>   Open daily, 10am-5pm
>   Entrance fee (grounds pass with one tour ticket)
> $10/adult; guided tours must be purchased
>   24 hours in advance

Trip 37 – Hiking an Historic Canal and Touring an Historic House

WHY: Discover the history of a 19th century ill-fated canal project, now enshrouded in vegetation, and contrast it with 18th century-built Sully, so well-kept that it looks like the family just left for the day.

WHERE: From the Beltway take SR7 toward Leesburg and get off at Lansdowne Blvd. (SR2400), setting your app for Bazil Newman Riverfront Park. Park there and enjoy the hike along the Potomac River. Go to a different section of the Park (43942 Riverpoint Drive) where you can hike and also learn lots of history about Goose Creek. Drive back to Ford's Fish Shack for lunch. Get back on SR7 and turn off on SR28 to Sully.

HOW LONG: It will take about a half hour to get to Riverfront Park from the Capital Beltway. Several hours of hiking divided between the two sites will work up an appetite for lunch, only 5 minutes away. Sully is about 20 minutes from the lunch strop. Spend the rest of the afternoon there. Take the docent-guided tour of the house or follow maps from the Visitor Center to the outbuildings and archaeological remains.

LUNCH BREAK: Ford's Fish Shack (19308 Promenade Dr. Lansdowne) is a popular maritime-themed seafood spot. Our favorites are the fish tacos and lobster rolls.

HIGHLIGHTS: Bazil Newman Riverfront Park offers you grand views of the Potomac River and the little islands that are perches for black cormorants and blue herons. If you drag your kayak down to the riverside, you will experience only calm, flat water. At the next section of the park that we visited, you can explore the remains of two historical events: The Goose Creek and Little River Navigation Company and the pontoon bridge that carried Union General Joseph

Hooker's Army of the Potomac across the river at Edwards Ferry in pursuit of General Lee's Army. The Canal company began in 1830 but had problems raising capital and faced growing doubts about canal travel vs. rail. The deserted village of Elizabeth Mills and the canal's stone ruins, including massive double locks, are the only relics left. The company managed to complete the locks and four canals by the close of 1851. Ground grain from the mills could now be floated to the C&O Canal, a little more than a mile away, but sandbars began to build up and enslaved labor had to drag the boats across. Investment funds dried up. The second event was before the battle at Gettysburg, over three days in 1863, when nearly 80,000 infantrymen, 12,000 cavalry-men, 379 pieces of artillery and 3,000 supply wagons crossed the Potomac there during the run-up to Gettysburg. The historic marker at the parking lot tells the story.

Sully Historic House was built during 1793-95 for Richard Bland Lee, Northern Virginia's first Congressman. It is now owned by Fairfax County's Park Authority with a permanent lease on the land from Dulles Airport. Airport plans in 1959 were to tear down 300 homes as a buffer zone, and Sully was one of them. Quick action by concerned citizens saved it. It is furnished as if the Lees were still the owners, but many families lived there following the departure of the Lees for Washington DC in 1811. They included a Lee cousin, several families of Quakers from New York state, a local dairy farmer who made highly acclaimed cheese, and two diplomats. They all took loving care of the property, so much so that the floors, doors, hardware and most of the glass are original. Now Sully serves as a tangible link to the past. Site programs include house tours and a tour of the outbuildings, including the enslaved cabin built with period techniques and tools on the footprint of the original. Special programs are designed for school children and Boy and Girl Scouts, and popular events are held on the property, including the Father's Day car show.

MORE INFORMATION

Bazil Newman Riverfront Park
    www.loudoun.gov>Bazil_Newman_Riverfront_Park
    (Named for a Black entrepreneur who operated a
        ferry on the site in the 19th century)

Sully Historic House
    www.fairfaxcounty.gov/parks/sull-historic-site
    3650 Historic Sully Way, Chantilly
    703-437-1794
    House open for tours Thursday-Sunday, 11am,
        1pm, and 3pm
    Outbuilding tours: Thursday-Sunday, 2pm
    Entrance fee $10/adult, $8/senior

Trip 38 – Biking the W&OD to a Botanical Wonderland

WHY: Bike another section of the fascinating W&OD and take a detour built just for bikes to 95 acres of landscaped gardens, a restored 18th century log cabin and one of a kind Korean Bell Garden.

WHERE: Start biking at mile 17 on Sunset Hills, Reston and ride a few miles until you see the connector trail to Meadowlark Botanical Gardens. Visit the Gardens and get back on the Trail to the middle of Vienna where you can buy your lunch at Whole Foods on Maple Ave., eating it in a little seating area behind the store on the trail. Then go as far as you want on the trail before heading back to your car.

LUNCH BREAK: See above.

HOW LONG: Spend the morning at Meadowlark and ride on the WO&D Bike trail until your legs give out.

HIGHLIGHTS: **Meadowlark Botanical Gardens** began as the 74-acre farm in Virginia's rolling Piedmont that economist Gardiner Means and social historian Caroline Ware bought in 1935. They lived there over the next 50 years and then donated their beloved farm to the Northern Virginia Regional Park Authority. NVRPA then bought a contiguous 21-acre parcel. By the mid-80s, three lakes were added to the largest stream course as well as several trails. Meadowlark opened officially in 1987. It is now unparalelled in the Washington Area as a public garden.

Meadowlark has identifed the Potomac River Valley as a geographic province that determines which native plants are accessed. Cherry blossoms abound in the spring. Lake Carolyn is stocked with koi and turtles that visitors can watch from a bridge and gazebo. The Korean Bell Garden is the only one of its kind in the Western Hemisphere. Many Korean images as well as images symbolic of Virginia can be seen on the traditional Korean stuctures. At the top of the hill the pagoda houses a huge Korean bell. There are many special events at the gardens, including a Winter Walk of Lights in December. Meadowlark has 3.5 miles of paved trails.

The W&O Railroad Regional Park, the "skinniest park in Virginia" includes many interesting things to see and historical events to learn about. Keep your eyes pealed for the many historical markers along your route. Today, only 8 stations that served the W&OD trains remain. You will pass by one, the Vienna station that is leased to the Northern Virginia Model Railroaders Association, which runs it as a model train operation. Freeman House, beside the trail on Church Street in Vienna, served as a hospital during the Civil War and is open to the public as a general store, selling cold drinks and W&OD history books. If you go as far as Falls Church, you will use the Route 7 Overpass. Route 7 was originally part of a long trail of the Algonkian and Sioux Indians, and later became a stagecoach route between Leesburg and Alexandria.

MORE INFORMATION

Meadowlark Botanical Gardens
     www.novaparks.com/parks/meadowlark-botanical-
        gardens
     9750 Meadowlark Gardens Ct., Vienna
     703-255-3631
     Open April-October, 10am-4pm
        November-March, 10am-3:30pm
     Entrance fee $6/adult, $3/children and seniors
     Paper maps no longer available; scan QR code
        onsite

Washington & Old Dominion Railroad Regional Park
     www.novaparks.com
     Open daily, 5am-9pm

Trip 39 – On the Water and in the Town of Lord Fairfax

WHY: Paddling on the Occoquan Reservoir in a wilderness filled with heron and kingfishers seems incongruous right next door to a suburban landscape. A short distance away is historic Fairfax, a Civil War crossroads where an old farmhouse—next to a civil war interpretive center—hides a wealth of graffiti by young soldiers.

WHERE: From the Capital Beltway, take I-95 south and then SR123 north toward Occoquan. In four and a half miles, turn left onto Hampton Road. In about three miles, turn left into Fountainhead Regional Park. After boating, return to SR123 and continue north into the city of Fairfax. Turn right on Main Street and immediately to the left is the lunch stop. After lunch, continue on Main Street for three blocks to the Fairfax Museum on the right where you can pick up a walking tour map. To get to the interpretive center, go back on Main Street and turn right at Old Lee Highway. A few blocks after the second light you will see the entrance to Blenheim (the old farmhouse) and the interpretive center on the left.

HOW LONG: It will take 30 minutes to get from the Capital Beltway to Fountainhead. A six-mile loop around the reservoir took us two hours. A bare 15 minutes should get you to lunch, and the museum and interpretive center are only minutes away.

LUNCH BREAK: Avoid the conventional chains in Fairfax City and go to the little **Havabite Eatery**, which has been at the same location at 10416 Main Street for 30 years. Havabite is in one of the oldest commercial buildings in Fairfax. It is Greek/Italian with tasty gyro sandwiches and outstanding onion rings.

HIGHLIGHTS: **Fountainhead Regional Park**'s Occoquan Reservoir furnishes the water supply for Alexandria and Fairfax County. Upriver divides into the Occoquan River on the left and Bull Run on the right. Paddle upriver—to the right—from the boat ramp. You'll see plenty of heron and kingfishers. If you don't want to go more than six miles, turn around at the point where the two rivers divide. Otherwise, you can go two miles further and reach Bull Run Marina at the Old Yates Ford Bridge where there is a snack bar and restrooms. This is also on NOVA Park's longest natural surface trail (at 19.6 miles), the Bull Run-Occoquan hiking trail.

The **Fairfax Museum**, located in the oldest schoolh o u s e in the county, is a modest affair but outlines the proud history of the area. Fairfax's colonial beginnings arose from an unbelievably huge land grant—over five million acres—

awarded to Thomas Fairfax, 6th Lord Fairfax. Pick up the walking map, which covers only six square blocks but more than 200 years of American history. On the tour route is the Fairfax County Courthouse, which houses the treasured wills of George and Martha Washington. On June 1, 1861, the first heavy engagement of the Civil War occurred here, the Confederate flag was designed here, and Mosby's Rangers, in a daring raid here, captured a Union general, 32 other soldiers and 58 horses. The nearby **Civil War Interpretive Center** tells the story of the Civil War in Fairfax County and has on its grounds a house that was occupied by Union soldiers soon after it was built. Its walls are covered in graffiti, "a diary on walls," and the fragile writings in the attic have been lovingly recreated life-sized in the center. A short informative video plays all day. Take the house tour and walk the secluded 12-acre grounds, viewing interpretive signage along groomed pathways.

MORE INFORMATION

Fountainhead Regional Park
www.novaparks.com/parks/fountainhead-
  regional-park
10875 Hampton Road, Fairfax Station
703-250-9124
Open daily, dawn-dusk
Boat ramp launch fee $5/adults, $2.50/seniors
Canoe, kayak, and jon boat rental available at
  start of 19.6-mile hiking trail to Bull Run
  Regional Park
Entrance free

Fairfax Museum and Visitor Center
www.fairfaxva.gov/government/historic-resources
10209 Main Street, Fairfax
703-385-8414
Open daily, 11am-4pm
Self-guided walking tour map available
Entrance free

Civil War Interpretive Center at Historic Blenheim
www.fairfaxva.gov/government/historic-
  resources/civil-war-interpretive-center
3610 Old Lee Highway, Fairfax
703-591-0560
Open Tuesday-Saturday, 1pm; tours limited to 7
  people
Entrance free

Trip 40 – Hike through Manassas National Battlefield Park with a Side Trip to the Manassas Museum

WHY: Almost unchanged from the time of the two major Civil War battles fought here (First Manassas was the first of the Civil War), the tranquil countryside bore witness to war's hell, amply illustrated in the Visitor Center. The town of Manassas has a state-of-the-art museum in its Victorian center that focuses on the Civil War period.

WHERE: Take I-66 West from the Capital Beltway to Manassas Exit 47B and follow Business Route 234 north a short distance to the park entrance. After hiking, take SR234 back into Manassas, passing all the fast foods to reach the center of the old town.

HOW LONG: An easy 5.4 mile hike following the First Manassas Trail takes two and a half hours. Add an hour each for the Battlefield Visitor Center, lunch, and then a few hours for the Manassas Museum.

LUNCH BREAK: Eat lunch on the way from the Battlefield to the museum at **Cracker Barrel** (10801 Battleview Parkway), only a smidgin above a fast food, but it's conveniently located.

HIGHLIGHTS: Start your hike in **Manassas National Battlefield Park** at the statue of General Thomas J. (Stonewall) Jackson after viewing the excellent exhibits at the Visitor Center. The main exhibit re-enacts the fighting at First Manassas (Bull Run) with a map, moving lights, and a 45-minute video. The hiking route is easy to follow with blue-blazed wooden stakes at most decision points. The trail is unusually varied in terrain— through meadows, along the edge of and through evergreen forests, beside Bull Run, and past houses and ruins that witnessed the battles. The only confusing part is at the Van Pelt house. Do not go straight ahead but go to the right to a few information markers and then down the hill toward US29. Walk along a new and very long boardwalk above a little swamp, and you'll see the picturesque Stone Bridge over Bull Run. It was rebuilt in 1880 after being destroyed in 1862 by the war. Take the path before the bridge to the left, and a little further on you can still see the actual scars left on the bank where Sherman's troops crossed to join the battle on Matthews Hill. Go up the hill and you rejoin the blue-blazed path. At the end of the hike, if you haven't experienced enough history, you can drive the 16-mile tour of the Second Manassas Battlefield. A map for the driving tour is available in the Visitor Center.

After lunch, visit the newly renovated **Manassas Museum**. Built in 1991, it has an award- winning short video called "A Community at War" that describes the settlement of the area and the legacy of the Civil War. Historic artifacts and photographs corroborate this story. It also invites you to a self-guided field trip that explores three different important historic sites in Manassas that showcase the important contributions of African American residents of the city. This includes Liberia House, where over 80 enslaved people worked on one of the largest plantations in Northern Virginia, and the house where the former enslaved Jennie Dean founded the Manassas Industrial School for Colored Youth in 1893; Frederick Douglass conducted the opening ceremony.

MORE INFORMATION

Manassas National Battlefield Park
www.nps.gov/mana
6511 Sudley Road, Manassas
703-361-1339
Open daily, 8:30am-5pm
Entrance free

Manassas City
www.manassascity.org

Manassas Museum
www.manassasmuseum.org
9101 Prince William Street, Manassas
703-368-1873
Open Monday-Saturday, 10am-5pm
    Sunday, 12pm-5pm
Entrance free

Trip 41 – Morning Hike on the Slopes of the Blue Ridge and the Afternoon in Warrenton

WHY: G. Richard Thompson Wildlife Management Area is renowned in the spring for its showy stands of white trillium, reputed to be the largest on the east coast. Warrenton is the quaint county seat of Fauquier County and a mecca for horse lovers. The Old Jail Museum is fun, believe it or not.

WHERE: Take I-66 west from the Capital Beltway and get off at Markham, Exit 18. Take SR55 to Linden and turn right onto Freezeland Road for about 6 miles to the WMA parking lot on the right just before Trillium Trail Road on the left. After your hike, go back to I-66 and turn off on US17 south toward Warrenton. Turn right on Meetze Road (county 643) and then right onto North Falmouth Street, which becomes Main Street. The restaurant and Old Jail are both on Main Street. Return on I-66.

HOW LONG: The drive to the WMA takes about an hour from the Capital Beltway. The four and a half-mile hike took us two hours. The ride to Warrenton takes about 25 minutes. Eat lunch and enjoy exploring the town in the afternoon.

LUNCH BREAK: Eat lunch at **Black Bear Bistro** (32 Main Street), which is famous for its bulging sandwiches, hearty vegan chili, and brick oven pizza at very reasonable prices.

HIGHLIGHTS: G. Richard Thompson Wildlife Management Area is a mecca for hunters, fishermen and hikers. The man himself was an avid hunter who saw to it that this 4,000 acre tract of land was donated to the state of Virginia. You can do the whole circular hike of 9.2 miles, starting at Thompson Lake on the northeast side, or a less taxing route along the Appalachian Trail (AT) at the top of the mountain on the northwest side, which we did. The latter gets you to the wildflowers faster without the steep climb or muddy path. From the WMA parking lot described above, head downhill to the intersection with the AT (white blazed). Go either right, left or both ways on the AT to see the Trillium, Lady Slippers and Showy Orchis. These are at their peak  at the beginning of May. Look also for the occasional beautiful vistas.

After lunch, visit the **Old Jail Museum** in Warrenton, one of the most perfectly preserved old jails in the Commonwealth. Built in 1808, its four small cells were each approved to house 40 prisoners. In 1823 the jail was converted to a house for the jailer, and a new stone jail was built complete with hanging/exercise yard. Now the home of the Fauquier Historical Society, it features exhibits of Revolutionary and Civil War artifacts, Col. John S. Mosby memorabilia, a Rappahannock canal boat, and an old wine cellar from a Fauquier winery, the first in the state. Warrenton was first settled in 1759 as Red Store and grew up as a crossroads town. It was a hospital town during the Civil War. Its claim to fame is as the birthplace of John Marshall, fourth Chief Justice of the Supreme Court. To the horsey set, it is famous as the site of the Warrenton Horse Show and the Virginia Gold Cup Race.

MORE INFORMATION

G. Richard Thompson Wildlife Management Area
dwr.virginia.gov/vbwt/sites/g-richard-thompson-
wildlife-managment-area
Alltrails.com suggests 6 great trails for birding and
hiking along with maps, reviews, and photos

Warrenton
www.warrentonva.gov

**Old Jail Museum (now the home of the Fauquier
Historical Society)**
fauquierhistory.org
10 Ashby Street, Warrenton
540-347-5525
Open Wednesday-Monday, 11am-4pm
Entrance fee $5/adult, $4/senior

Trip 42 – Visit to Museum of the Shenandoah and Hike at Sky Meadows State Park

WHY: Visit a spectacular museum celebrating the beautiful Shenandoah Valley and then take a hike that one travel writer claims will give you "one of the best grand-stand views in northern Virginia."

WHERE: Take I-66 west from the Capital Beltway and then I-81 north, turning off at Exit 310. Follow signs for SR37 north and then US50 (Winchester/Romney exit). Turn right onto US50/Amherst Street. Eat lunch in town (US50 becomes Cork Street). To get to Sky Meadows, return on US50 east and go south on SR17, turning right at SR710. After hiking, continue on US50 for a ride through Virginia hunt country on the way home.

HOW LONG: The trip to and from Winchester takes about an hour each way. Allow two to three hours for the museum. A circular hike of five miles at Sky Meadows takes about two and a half hours.

LUNCH BREAK: The museum only offers snacks, so we tried the **Cork Street Tavern** in Winchester (8 W. Cork Street, Rt. 50), advertised as "casual American dining."

HIGHLIGHTS: A visit to the **Museum of the Shenandoah** includes not only the museum, but an ancestral home, gardens, and an art park. Beautifully designed by renowned architect Michael Graves, the museum houses three galleries for permanent collections and one gallery for changing exhibitions. Its signature gallery tells the story of the Valley from its Paleolithic Indian past to today's eclectic mix of people. Other galleries contain a huge collection of miniature doll houses and the paintings, furniture and decorative art of the original owner of the **Glen**

Burnie Historic House. The house is just as it was furnished by Julian Wood Glass Jr., last descendent of Winchester's founder to live in the house.

Six acres of gardens surround the Glen Burnie House and include small intimate gardens as well as a large Grand Allee. A new feature is a free-admission art park on 90 acres, called "The Trails at the MSV". It features outdoor art installations and miles of trails through fields, woods, and wetlands, which allow dogs on leash.

After lunch, drive a short way to **Sky Meadows State Park** in Delaplane. The land was saved from development by a 1,500 acre purchase and gift of Paul Mellon. It even includes a tract that was purchased from Lord Fairfax by George Washington. Generations of farming have made for an interesting blend of pasture and woodlands, which allows for unparalleled views of the deep blue hills and a blaze of colorful foliage in the fall. The Mount Bleak house, finished in 1850 by a local farmer, has been recently restored to its original appearance and offers tours (call for hours). The park has an excellent variety of programs throughout the year; October festival days include a pumpkin patch and local wine tasting. The park is particularly well marked with loop trails and others that can be combined for hikes of one to five miles, and one trail intersects with the Appalachian Trail. The five-miler includes some hard climbs, but the views are worth it. The park has been designated as an International Dark Sky Park and holds monthly astronomy programs.

MORE INFORMATION

Museum of the Shenandoah Valley
www.themsv.org
901 Amherst Street, Winchester
540-662-1473
Open Tuesday-Sunday, 10am-5pm
Entrance fee $15/adult, $10/senior for museum,
house and gardens

Sky Meadows State Park
www.dcr.virginia.gov/state_parks/sky meadows
11012 Edmonds Lane, Delaplane
540-592-3556
Open daily, 8am-dusk
Entrance fee $10/vehicle on weekdays
Good map on website "Sky Meadows State Park
Trails"

Trip 43 – Skyline Hike: Plain or Fancy

NOTE: This trip comes in two versions—hence plain or fancy. The first includes a leisurely hike to Mary's Rock, enjoying a packed lunch along the trail, a scenic 30-mile drive north on the Skyline Drive to Front Royal, and home via I-66. The second requires arrival at the hike's start early enough to be completed by around noon, when you eat your packed lunch, followed by a drive to Belle Grove Plantation and Cedar Creek in Middletown.

VERSION 1

WHY: This trail is spectacularly scenic throughout its length, not just at the climactic 360-degree view at the top. It is a good introduction to our second nearest National Park (after Great Falls Park).

WHERE: From the Capital Beltway, take I-66 west and then US29/211 west to Warrenton. Turn right in town on US211 and follow the signs to Thornton Gap. Just past Skyline Drive, turn left into a parking lot where there are well-maintained bathrooms. The trailhead to Mary's Rock starts from the turnaround circle at the end of the upper parking lot. In the woods, turn almost immediately left at the T-intersection and follow the trail to **Mary's Rock**. When you near the summit, the Appalachian Trail turns left, but you continue straight ahead to the Rock. Return to your car and follow the Skyline Drive for 30 miles to Front Royal, stopping at the **Dickey Ridge Visitor Center** along the way (restrooms, exhibits, video, gift shop). There are spectacular views along the way from both sides. At the northern terminus of the park, follow US340 through Front Royal where it connects with I-66.

HOW LONG: The distance to Skyline Drive is 70 miles and

takes only about one and a half hours as you will be going against traffic. The Park Service estimates that the round-trip hike to Mary's Rock (3.6 miles) takes three and a half hours—a very leisurely pace. The drive north on Skyline Drive to the park entrance takes about an hour because the speed limit, strictly enforced, is only 35mph. The distance from Front Royal back to the Beltway via I-95 is 62 miles and should be easy as you will again be driving against traffic.

LUNCH BREAK: Pack a good-sized lunch with liquids. The climb up is strenuous.

HIGHLIGHTS: **Shenandoah National Park**, established in 1935, is only 75 miles from DC but is the proverbial world away. The Blue Ridge Mountains were formed over a billion years ago and eroded over millennia to form today's tranquil hills and hollows. After the Europeans arrived, many hundreds of homesteads were built, minerals were mined, and mountainsides were logged, scarring the land. By the beginning of the twentieth century there were calls for protection, but it was decades before the park was authorized and over 450 families moved outside the park. In 1928, when private purchase was still allowed, President Hoover and his wife Lou bought a plot within the park to be their

summer White House, which they called Rapidan Camp. The Civilian Conservation Corps, formed during the Great Depression, helped build many of the park's facilities and roads. The Park has over 500 miles of trails, including 101 miles of the Appalachian Trail. The trail to Mary's Rock gains its 1,240 feet of elevation on a well-graded switch-backed pathway, often wide enough for two people.

VERSION 2

WHY: In addition to a spectacular hike in Shenandoah National Park, visits to Belle Grove Manor House and Cedar Creek Battlefield introduce you to the rich cultural heritage of the Shenandoah Valley and a decisive Civil War battle.

WHERE: The directions are the same as VERSION 1 until after the hike. Instead of taking the Skyline Drive, go west on US211, turning north on US340. Go through Front Royal, and just past I-66, turn left on Reliance Road (SR627) and then left again on US11 into Middletown. Belle Grove Plantation is on your right and Cedar Creek Battlefield Visitor Center is on your left. After your visits, retrace your steps to I-66 and turn east toward DC.

HOW LONG: We climbed to Mary's Rock and back (3.6 miles) in two and a half hours—one hour less than the leisurely Park Service estimate. This was at a steady pace, but we also stopped for frequent pictures and a snack. After the hike, eat your lunch in a scenic spot, and the drive to Middletown can take at least 45 minutes depending on traffic in Front Royal. Visits to both sites take about two hours.

LUNCH BREAK: On your own.

HIGHLIGHTS: (See VERSION 1 for **Shenandoah National Park** highlights.) **Belle Grove Plantation**, owned by the National Trust for Historic Preservation, was built by Revolutionary War patriot Major Isaac Hite in 1797. He married President James Madison's sister Nelly. Madison often visited Belle Grove, and President Thomas Jefferson helped design the house, which was built of limestone quarried nearby. The original house on the property was built in 1731 by Hite's father, one of many German immigrants to the valley. Once the centerpiece of a 7,500-acre plantation, the historic site now includes the original icehouse and smokehouse, an enslaved cemetery, and an early twentieth century barn, all set against a beautiful mountain backdrop. A tour of the house is offered on demand.

On October 19, 1864, Belle Grove stood at the center of the Civil War battle of **Cedar Creek**. The Shenandoah Valley played a strategic role in the Civil War. A daring dawn surprise attack by 14,000 Confederate troops under the command of Gen. Jubal Early seemingly routed 30,000 federal troops, but Union Gen. Philip Sheridan rallied his scattered troops to a counterattack and victory for the North. The battle marked the end of the 1864 Valley Campaign, contributed to Abraham Lincoln's reelection as President, and was the ultimate Union victory. The Battle of Cedar Creek is reenacted each year in October. Cedar Creek and Belle Grove were established as a National Historical Park in 2002. The Battlefield Visitor Center in Middletown (7712 Main Street), operated by the Cedar Creek Battlefield Foundation, has a few exhibits and a guide to a one mile interpretive trail of the earthworks.

MORE INFORMATION

Shenandoah National Park
   www.nps.gov/shen
   3655 Hwy 211 East, Luray
   540-999-3500
   Open generally April-November, but check
      schedule on website for details by area
   Entrance fee $30/vehicle

Belle Grove Plantation
   bellegrove.org
   336 Belle Grove Road, Middletown
   540-869-2028
   Open March 18-end of October
   Monday-Saturday, 10am-4pm
   Sunday, 1pm-5pm, tours begin 15 minutes after the
      hour; see site for winter hours
   Entrance fee $14/adult, $13/senior

Cedar Creek Battlefield Foundation
   www.nps.gov/cebe/index.htm
   8437 Valley Pike, Middletown
   540-869-2064
   Open April 1-October 30, Thursday-Monday,
      1pm-5pm
   Entrance free

Trip 44 – Hiking Shenandoah Park from the Eastern Side

WHY: You don't have to start from the Skyline Drive to find wonderful hikes and beautiful views in the park. Climb the challenging Little Devil's Stairs from the east side of the park and visit the curious little towns near the starting point.

WHERE: From the Capital Beltway, take I-66 west and then US29/211 west to Warrenton. Turn right in town on US211 and follow the road to the foothills of the park. The little towns of Flint Hill, Washington, and Sperryville are all on US522, which is north of and then contiguous with US211. After exploring the towns and eating lunch, go back to US211, turning west, and then take SR622 (Gid Brown Hollow Road) for about two miles. Turn left on SR614 (Keyser Run Road) for four miles, dead-ending at the trailhead.

HOW LONG: The distance to Sperryville from the Beltway is 63 miles and takes about one and a quarter hours. Cruising the little towns and perhaps touring the distillery or winery could take at least an hour. After lunch, the hike takes <u>at least</u> three and a half hours. The first part is 2.2 miles, mostly uphill, and the fire road back to the trailhead is 3.3 miles. You can go a few miles back to Sperryville for ice cream at **Burgers N Things** (12000 Lee Highway; Sperryville) before retracing your route home.

LUNCH BREAK: **Griffin Tavern** in Flint Hill (659 Zachary Taylor Highway) is three miles north of US211 on US522. It features home- style meals and pub favorites such as fish 'n chips and shepherd's pie. The tavern is in an attractive old house on a flower-covered hill.

HIGHLIGHTS: **Little Devil's Stairs** is a spectacular and strenuous hike, climbing 1,480 feet up along a rocky gorge. Giant rocks form the staircase, hence the name. Look for the blue blazes on the trees going up and the yellow blazes along the fire road coming down, but getting lost is not a problem. The trail is most beautiful in the spring when the waterfalls are at their peak. However, the water fords are deepest at this time and the rocks slippery and dangerous. Personally, we prefer to hike the dry trail in the summer when the area is at least 10 degrees cooler than inside the Beltway. Carry plenty of water with you. The beautiful views are largely along the trail of the steep cliffs with the waterfalls on either side, but coming back along the fire road, there is a glimpse of the sublime blue foothills.

Sperryville is a tiny town that had its heyday long ago and is now home to several artists' studios and **Copper Fox Distillery and Antiques**. The distillery malts its own barley and makes applewood- aged single malt American whiskey and rye whiskey. **Washington** (known as Little Washington to distinguish it from its big cousin), is the county seat of Rappahannock County. The area was owned by Thomas Fairfax, 6th Lord Fairfax, who hired 16-year-old George Washington, a distant relative, to survey his lands west of the Blue Ridge Mountains. On July 24, 1749, the town layout as it appears today was surveyed and platted by Washington and his two assistants. The town was relatively unaffected by the Industrial Age and thus the current town is

refreshingly similar to the one of 150 years ago. The town is best known for The Inn at Little Washington, a five-star restaurant and inn that has won numerous national awards. For wine lovers, the family-owned **Gadino Cellars** provides   samples   of   their winemaking art in their Italian style tasting room or on their spacious deck overlooking vines and gardens.

MORE INFORMATION

Wasmund's Copper Fox Distillery
   www.copperfoxdistillery.com
   9 River Lane, Sperryville
   540-987-8554
   Open daily, 10am-8pm
   Tours $10/person
      Tour and classic whisky flight $18/person

Gadino Cellars
   www.gadinocellars.com
   92 Schoolhouse Road, Washington
   540-987-9292
   Tasting room hours: Friday, 11:30am-5pm
      Saturday, 11:30am-6pm
      Sunday and Monday, 11:30am-5pm
      Individual tasting fees - $12/flight
      2 free tastings with purchase of 3 bottles

Trip 45 – From Dinosaur Tracks to a Boutique Vineyard in Lord Culpeper's Land Grant

WHY: Having biked through vineyards in France, we can attest that Culpeper offers just as many gentile delights—from pedaling through bucolic countryside to a lunch inspired by European country cooking—all amid an historic landscape of dinosaurs and Civil War battles.

WHERE: From the Capital Beltway, take I-66 west (Exit 49) for 22 miles. Turn off at Exit 43A, Gainesville, and follow US 29 west and then south to Culpeper—about 35 miles. Follow the signs through town to the Visitor Center. Take the walking tour through town and to the restaurant. Then start biking from the Visitor Center left on Davis Street. and then left on S. East Street, continuing left on Chandler and left on Keyser. Go right on SR667, right on SR666, and right on SR663. Turn right on Corkys Lane and follow the Old House Vineyard signs. When you leave the vineyard, turn right on SR663 and turn east toward Culpeper on SR3 for about seven miles. Go back to the Visitor Center and then retrace your steps by car along US29 and I-66 to the Beltway.

HOW LONG: It takes about 1 hour 15 minutes to get to Culpeper's Visitor Center from the Beltway. The walking tour, visit to the museum, and a leisurely lunch took us about two and a half hours. The round-trip bike trip to the vineyard is 16½ miles and took us just two hours, including a stop at the tasting room.

LUNCH BREAK: **It's About Thyme** (128 E. Davis Street) rates right up there in gastronomic bliss with the little inns in Provence. It also has a raw bar in the neighboring building and a wonderful deli/pastry shop. We had turkey in puff pastry and an open-faced ham sandwich with béchamel sauce, accompanied by an exquisitely fresh greens salad. The place was packed; a reservation is recommended if you stay for dinner.

HIGHLIGHTS: **Culpeper Visitor Center** in the historic Train Depot is the place to start— maps customized to your taste and a superb free book of walking and driving tours that even includes an architectural glossary. We took the S. East Street walk, one of Culpeper's most historically significant streets. The street contains many fine homes and a wide variety of architectural styles—both ante- and post-bellum. The walk includes the **Museum of Culpeper History** where you'll first see displayed 215-million-year-old dinosaur tracks found in a nearby quarry. An interactive map helps you trace the County's timeline from life in a Manahoac Village to the first settlements in Lord Culpeper's gargantuan land grant that extended to present-day Fairfax County, and the many Civil War Battles that raged in and around the town. The town's fortune and misfortune has been its strategic location at the confluence of the Rapidan and Rappahannock Rivers. You can top off your visit by visiting the **Burgandine House** next door, a log/plank cabin believed to be the oldest standing building in town.

The post-lunch bike ride takes you out of town by the Culpeper National Cemetery, originally established as a burial site for Union soldiers. It hosts over 200,000 visitors a year, many seeking warrior ancestors. The ride to **Old House Vineyard** (75 acres) goes through gently rolling countryside with beautiful views of the Blue Ridge Mountains. The 1800s farmhouse has been restored and is now the wine bar.

MORE INFORMATION

Culpeper Visitor Center
    www.culpeperva.gov
    111 S. Commerce Street, Culpeper
    540-727-0611
    Open year-round, Monday-Sunday, 10am-5pm

The Museum of Culpeper History
    www.culpepermuseum.com
    113 S. Commerce Street, Culpeper
    540-829-1749
    Open Monday-Sunday, 10am-4pm
    Guided tours can be scheduled
    Entrance fee—$5/adult, $4/senior

Old House Vineyard
    www.oldhousevineyards.com
    18351 Corkeys Lane, Culpeper
    540-423-1032
    Tasting room hours Monday, Wednesday,
        Thursday, and Friday, noon-5pm
        Saturday, 11am 6pm
        Sunday, noon-5pm

Trip 46 – Exploring Nature and History in the Mason Neck Peninsula

WHY: The Mason Neck Peninsula encompasses 1,813 acres, which include Gunston Hall, the home of George Mason—father of the Bill of Rights—and a beautiful Potomac shoreline. Bike, hike, or boat along the quiet waters that are home to a large population of American Bald Eagles and an additional 200 species of birds.

WHERE: From the Capital Beltway, take I-95 south to Exit 161 (Woodbridge). Follow US1 north, turning right at the light onto Gunston Road (SR 242). Mason Neck State Park is about five miles down the road on the right. Returning along this road, Gunston Hall is on the right.

HOW LONG: The drive south to the Peninsula takes about an hour. We spent about two hours kayaking on **Belmont Bay** and about the same time touring Gunston Hall.

LUNCH BREAK: There are no restaurants along Gunston Road. After a morning of boating, hiking, or biking, eat a packed picnic lunch before heading to Gunston Hall. Picnic tables are near the Environmental Center or just pull up your boat along the shoreline

HIGHLIGHTS: **Mason Neck Refuge** and **State Park**, adjacent to each other, occupy a parcel of land bought in 1967 to rehabilitate and preserve the habitat of the bald eagle and other animals that were endangered by logging and the use of the pesticide DDT. In addition to its healthy population of bald eagles, the area claims the largest great blue heron colony in the Mid-Atlantic, with some 600- 900 nests. The two preserves are a cornucopia of natural things to do. During the spring, summer, and fall, you can rent bicycles, canoes, and kayaks at the environmental center of the state park for a nominal fee. Boating silently up into the little coves of Belmont Bay, you are sure to see both water birds and raptors. You can also hike the one-mile Bayview Trail in the State Park or the three-mile Woodmarsh Trail in the Refuge where there are observation platforms over freshwater marshlands. The sounds of bullfrogs and turtles plopping into the water accompany you on your walk. Take bug spray. Mason Neck offers a full program of special events, including the Liz Hartwell Eagle Festival in April.

A short distance away, **Gunston Hall** was built in 1759 for George Mason and represents the work of the carpenter William Buckland and many indentured servants and enslaved. It sits high above the Potomac River and is a modest but elegant example of Georgian architecture, with hand-carved decorative moldings and bold colors on the wall that are true to the original. George Mason is one of the lesser-known American patriots, probably because he valued his privacy and held no public office. However, his ideas and writings were crucial for the birth of our country. In May 1776 he wrote the Virginia Declaration of Rights, which was the model for the US Bill of Rights. The Visitor Center offers an excellent orientation video and exhibits, and there is a guided mansion tour and a self-guided walk through the garden, outbuildings, and family burial ground. A nature trail leads down to the Potomac River.

```
┌─────────────────────────────────────────────────────┐
│                 MORE INFORMATION                      │
│                                                       │
│ Mason Neck State Park                                 │
│       www.dcr.virginia.gov/state-parks/masonneck      │
│       7301 High Point Road, Lorton                    │
│       703-339-2385                                    │
│       Open daily, 8am-dusk                            │
│       Entrance fee $10/car                            │
│                                                       │
│ Gunston Hall                                          │
│       www.gunstonhall.org/                            │
│       10709 Gunston Road, Mason Neck                  │
│       703-550-9220                                    │
│       Mansion and museum open daily, 9:30am-5pm       │
│           Guided tours at 10am, 11am, 1pm, 2pm, 3pm,  │
│           and 4pm                                     │
│       Entrance fee $10/adult, $8/senior               │
└─────────────────────────────────────────────────────┘
```

Trip 47 – Hiking in the Occoquan Bay National Wildlife Refuge and an Afternoon at the Workhouse Arts Center

WHY: Occoquan Bay National Wildlife Refuge is one of the largest remaining open spaces in Northern Virginia and provides a home and resting place for native and exotic birds. The Workhouse Arts Center is a phoenix rising out of the ashes of the former DC Workhouse and Reformatory.

WHERE: From the Capital Beltway, take US95 south to Exit 161 (Woodbridge), follow US1 south, cross the Occoquan River and turn left at the light onto Dawson Beach Road. The road ends at the Refuge. To get to Occoquan for lunch, go back to US1 north and turn left on US123, then left on Commerce Street. From Occoquan, turn left on US123 and cross the bridge to the Workhouse (Lorton) on the right.

HOW LONG: The drive south to the Refuge takes about three quarters of an hour, and both lunch and the workhouse are close by. You can easily spend two hours at each destination.

LUNCH BREAK: There are many lunch spots in Occoquan. We chose the **Blue Arbor Café** (201 Union Street) across from the Gaslight Landing townhomes. You might take the opportunity to explore the many shops.

HIGHLIGHTS: **Occoquan Bay National Wildlife Refuge** was established in 1998 after a former military research lab was turned over to the US Fish and Wildlife Service. The 644-acre refuge has a unique mix of wetlands, forest, and native grasslands that provide visitors with an opportunity to see over 650 species of plants, 220 species of birds, and 65 species of butterflies. Spring and fall are great times to observe migrating Neotropical birds and raptors. The refuge includes a one-mile wildlife drive and three miles of hiking trails (a good hiking map is available at the entry point). A nice circular trail goes from the parking lot around to Occoquan Bay and Painted Turtle Pond. We saw nesting ospreys and huge snapping turtles close to the trail.

The **Workhouse Arts Center** makes its home in the original red brick institutional setting of the prison, but the buildings have been gutted to provide sunlit airy studios for more than 150 artists. Each of the eight long former dormitories is devoted to a different art— ceramic, glass, painting, mixed media, and others— and a reception building provides information and changing exhibitions. The studio buildings each have their own galleries in the front, displaying the wares of the artists, and you can walk down the hall and observe art in the making at the studios. If you want to buy, there is a cashier at the front. The atmosphere is warm and welcoming, and what we thought would be a short visit turned into a two-hour feast for the eyes. On some

Saturdays on the quad is "Community Market" that displays the arts for sale and also has a food truck (CHEFIT) and free concerts. There is a wine festival in September. There is little to remind one of the site's past other than three aging watchtowers in one corner.

MORE INFORMATION

Occoquan Bay National Wildlife Refuge
    www.fws.gov/refuge/occoquan_bay
    13950 Dawson Beach Road, Woodbridge
    703-490-4979
    Open October 1-March 31, 7am-5pm
        April 1-September 30, 7am-7pm
    Entrance free

Workhouse Arts Center
    www.workhousearts.org
    9518 Workhouse Way, Lorton
    703-584-2900
    Open Wednesday-Saturday, 11am-6pm
        Sunday, noon-5pm

Trip 48 – Biking/Hiking/Rollerblading in Prince William Forest Park with a Side Visit to Occoquan

WHY: As the Park Ranger told us, Prince William Park is one of the best-kept secrets in the area—15,000 acres of woodland in deserted splendor (at least on the weekdays). Colorful birds, beaver, and wild turkey make their home here. Nearby Occoquan is a quaint little riverside town crowded with gift shops and eateries.

WHERE: From the Capital Beltway, take I-95 south for about 20 miles and exit on SR619 west. In only one half of a mile, turn right at the park entrance. After a morning of biking, hiking, or skating, head north on I-95 and then north on SR123. Turn left at the light onto Commerce Street into the town of Occoquan.

HOW LONG: The circular bike ride along the scenic drive of 12 miles is hilly and takes about one and a half hours or walk any of the 35 miles of hiking trails, each clearly marked on a map, which is free at the Visitor Center.

LUNCH BREAK: There are lots of restaurants in Occoquan; try The **Secret Garden Café** (404 Mill St.). It has "homemade dishes inspired by global cuisine."

HIGHLIGHTS: **Prince William Forest Park** was a major project of the Civilian Conservation Corps (CCC) during the 1930s after farming and mining had despoiled the land. During World War II it was home to the Office of Strategic Services (OSS), predecessor to the Central Intelligence Agency (CIA), where it trained spies and taught codes and covert radio transmission. The recovered thick woodland now protects four-fifths of the Quantico Creek watershed and is the largest example of a piedmont forest in the National Park System. It is a haven for wildlife and plants escaping urban sprawl. Half of the Park's scenic drive is one-way only, with half of that road reserved for non-vehicular traffic. You can hike, bike, or rollerblade there, one of the safest places for the latter sport in the area. In the winter you can even cross-country ski and snowshoe. Stop in the Visitor Center for a good historical look at the Indians who lived there when the colonists arrived and at exhibits of the pyrite mining operations and OSS activities.

Many bypass the town of **Occoquan** along I-95 without stopping, not realizing that there's much to enjoy. It was founded in 1750 as a port for shipping tobacco, grain, and fish, and in the 1800s was a popular weekend boating destination for DC residents. Then the town had a run of bad luck—a disastrous fire in 1919, the opening of Route 1 in 1929 that carried traffic away from the town, the silting-up of the river, a new railroad that bypassed the town and finally, Hurricane Agnes in 1972. Nevertheless, the townspeople persevered and repaired, rebuilt, and restored their town. It now features a large number and variety of historic homes and businesses, most of which have been in continuous use for over 100 years. Several of these old buildings are reportedly home to local ghosts; come on Halloween for a hair-raising tour. The residents have created a unique place that now offers shopping, antiquing, pleasant dining, and just a nice place to spend an afternoon.

MORE INFORMATION

Prince William Forest Park
    www.nps.gov/prwi
    18100 Park Headquarters Road, Triangle
    703-221-7181
    Open daily, sunrise-sunset
    Visitor Center open March 1-October 31, 9am-5pm
        November 1-February 28, 8am-4pm
    Good park maps on website
    Entrance fee $20/vehicle

Occoquan
    www.historicoccoquan.com
    At this site download a guide to the town's
        historical sites.

Trip 49 – Boating on a Quiet Inlet of the Potomac followed by a Visit with the Marines

WHY: During the week, Aquia Creek offers quiet, flat-water paddling for several miles before it enters the Potomac. Just up the road is the National Museum of the Marine Corps that honors servicemen whose exploits on the water were a bit more exciting. It is now the number one tourist attraction in Virginia, drawing 500,000 visitors annually.

WHERE: From the Capital Beltway, take I-95 south about 27 miles to Exit 140 east (SR630) toward Stafford. Turn left on SR1 and then take the second right on Hope Road. Follow Hope Road three and a half miles to the **Hope Springs Marina** sign and turn left into the Marina. For lunch after boating, ride north on SR1 and I-95 to Tun Tavern at the Marine Museum. It is only about seven miles from the Stafford exit, and it is clearly marked. Go home on I-95 north.

HOW LONG: From the Beltway, it takes only 30 minutes to get to the Hope Springs Marina in Stafford County. Paddling to the mouth of the Potomac and back in a leisurely fashion takes about two and a half hours. Lunch places along SR1 and at the Marine Museum are only minutes away from the Marina. The Museum is vast and, depending on your interest in things military, it can occupy an hour or all afternoon.

LUNCH BREAK: At the Marine Museum, you can eat in the "mess hall" or at **Tun Tavern** (seats 30), which is a re-creation of the eighteenth century public tavern in Philadelphia in which the first Colonial Marines were allegedly recruited in 1775.

HIGHLIGHTS: **Aquia Creek** is a tributary of the tidal segment of the Potomac River. The White House was built largely using sandstone quarried from Aquia Creek from 1792 to 1799. During the Civil War in 1861 (the Battle of Aquia Creek), three US gunships fired on a battery garrison during the Union campaign to blockade the Chesapeake Bay. Now the Creek provides a good mixture of activity typical for a little inlet along the Potomac—many nesting ospreys, private marinas with vast storage space and some really large yachts, an old railroad bridge with frequent long trains, green shoreline along park land, and a range of home styles—from ostentatious to modest. Go along the south bank (but not too close because there are thick green weeds) toward the mouth of the Potomac, enabling you to tie up at Aquia Landing Park for a rest. Go around the bend to the sandy beach on the Potomac as there are rocks on the Aquia Creek side. Return on the north side for a change of scenery.

The **National Museum of the Marine Corps** opened in 2006, and it is impressive both inside and out. A soaring ceiling reminiscent of the Air and Space Museum on the Mall suspends naval aircraft, and the museum flows easily in a chronologic manner from the Revolution to the present-day war against terrorism. Particularly interesting are the displays on the many US colonial wars that the Marines helped fight in far-flung regions of the globe including almost every Central American country and the former Spanish territories of the Philippines and Cuba. Did you know that battling Seminoles in Florida was once a part of the Marines' mission? The Museum tells the Marines' story well through the display of artifacts, multimedia, and full immersion experiences.

MORE INFORMATION

Hope Springs Marina
    www.hopespringsmarina.com
    4 Hope Springs Lane, Stafford
    540-659-1128
    $20 ramp fee for car-top boats; no kayak or
        canoe rental

National Museum of the Marine Corps
    www.usmcmuseum.org
    18900 Jefferson Davis Highway, Triangle
    877-635-1775
    Open daily, 9am-5pm except Christmas
        Docent-led tours for groups of 20 or fewer at
        10am and 2pm
    No entrance or parking fees

Trip 50 – Touring Fredericksburg's Civil War Parks and an Artist's Studio

WHY: Hiking at Spotsylvania Courthouse—one of the four major Civil War Battlefields surrounding Fredericksburg—allows you to imagine the nasty hand-to-hand combat that resulted in more than 30,000 casualties. Gari Melcher's home and studio high on the bluffs above the Rappahannock River is a soothing end to the day.

WHERE: From the Capital Beltway, take I-95 south to Fredericksburg and exit on US3 east, following signs to the Battlefield Visitor Center. Pick up the hiking map "Spotsylvania History Trail" and go to the Fredericksburg and Spotsylvania Military Parks. After your visit, go back to the city and have lunch on Caroline Street. To get to Melchers' Belmont, continue north on Caroline Street and follow your travel app.

HOW LONG: The drive to the Fredericksburg Visitor Center from the Beltway takes only 45 minutes, and the ride to Spotsylvania Court House takes another 15 minutes. The hike through the battlefield, depending on how many side paths you follow, will take two to three hours. After lunch, the drive to Belmont takes only 10 minutes. Reserve about two hours for the tour of the house and studio and for strolling in the gardens.

LUNCH BREAK: Eat at the **Fork-n-Biscuit** (715 Caroline St.) They serve brunch all day and claim they offer "quaint food from a time of yesteryear."

HIGHLIGHTS: **The Battle of Spotsylvania Court House** was fierce because this intersection controlled the shortest route to Richmond. Along with the other three major battles—Fredericksburg, Chancellorsville, and The Wilderness—no other area of comparable size witnessed such heavy and continuous fighting, with more than 100,000 casualties. It marked the beginning of the end for the South. The trail begins at the exhibit shelter and is marked by blue-blazed trees and mowed paths. The pleasant scenery alternates between open fields and shaded forests. It is permanently scarred by the honeycomb of trenches dug by both sides, which can still be clearly seen. The troops felled trees for additional protection. The worst carnage was at The Bloody Angle where the men fired into the faces of the enemy and stabbed at them with their bayonets through the crevices and holes between the logs. The other three battle sites are well worth another day's visit and have self-guided auto tours and walking trails.

Belmont was the home and studio of American artist Gari Melchers from 1916-32. The 27-acre estate was built in the 1790s and was untouched during the Civil War. Although relatively unknown today, Melchers was one of the most decorated artists of his day, both here and in Europe. He spent many years in the Netherlands where he painted realistic portraits of local customs and people. In his studio you can see some of these as well as portraits that he painted of Teddy Roosevelt and Mark Twain. His wife deeded the estate to the state of Virginia as a memorial to him, and all their lovingly collected furnishings are just as they left them. The boxwood walks and rose-covered arbors provide stunning views down to the river.

MORE INFORMATION

Fredericksburg and Spotsylvania National Military Park
    www.nps.gov/frsp
    Visitor Center: 1013 Lafayette Blvd.
    540-693-3200
    Park grounds open sunrise-sunset

Gari Melchers Home and Studio
    www.GariMelchers.org
    224 Washington Street, Falmouth
    540-654-1015
    Open 10am-5pm, tours offered hourly
        Gardens and trails available free 10am-5pm
    Entrance fee $12/adult; grounds free of charge

Trip 51 – Visits to George Washington Birthplace and Stratford, Home of the Lee Family

WHY: Two prominent American families—the Washingtons and Lees— established themselves in the 1700s here in the Northern Neck area of Virginia, just miles from each other's homes. A visit here makes clear the central role of Virginia and its planters in our country's founding.

WHERE: Take I-95 south off of the Capital Beltway and turn east on SR3 at Fredericksburg. Go to Stratford Hall first off SR3, following your app, and then on your return eat lunch at a funny little place in Montross before turning off SR 3 for Washington's Birthplace.

HOW LONG: The round-trip takes about three hours. Allow an additional hour for Washington Birthplace and at least two hours for Stratford. Both are designed for easy walking throughout.

LUNCH BREAK: Eat at **Bird Dogs Country Store** (10663 King's Hwy. Montross). Customers say it has "hot fresh food you can eat on picnic tables outside" but the soft shell crab sandwich convinced us to stop.

HIGHLIGHTS: **Stratford Hall** is the grand ancestral home of the Lees, including Revolutionary War hero "Light Horse Harry" Lee and his son, Civil War General Robert E. Lee, who was born there in 1807. It was also home to Richard Henry Lee and Francis Lightfoot Lee, the only two brothers to sign the Declaration of Independence. The truly handsome house, left undamaged by the Civil War, has been restored and meticulously preserved. Its Great Hall is often described as one of the most beautiful rooms in America. The expansive grounds include an excellent Visitor Center, facilities for special events and overnight stays (in cabins), nature trails, an old gristmill, and beautiful vistas from the bluffs overlooking the Potomac.

Stratford Hall has now automated its tours; self-guided tours are available that bring the social and cultural history of Stratford Hall to life. The topics of the Audio tours include Who lived at Stratford, Band of Brothers: The Lee Men of Stratford Hall, Leading Ladies: The Lee Women of Stratford Hall, and The Crossroads: African and African American Life at Stratford Hall.

George Washington Birthplace at Popes Creek is a National Monument that commemorates the birthplace of our first President. There is nothing left of the actual house where he lived until he was four years old, but a house built there in 1938 is close to the site and in keeping with the period architecture. The view along the Potomac River is as it was in Washington's day. Colonial farm buildings recreate the atmosphere of an eighteenth century, mid-sized tobacco farm. The area's distinctive Tidewater culture was a society in which Washington's father, grandfather, and great-grandfather before him were firmly entrenched. From this culture, Washington took on the traits which defined his character: his sense of public duty and his love of farming.

MORE INFORMATION

Stratford
> www.stratfordhall.org
> 483 Great House Road, Stratford
> 804-493-8038
> Open Wednesday-Sunday, 10am-5pm
> Only tours are audio tours
> Entrance fee $15/adult, $14/senior
> Tickets are required and may be purchased online
> > or at the Stratford Hall Gate House

George Washington Birthplace
> www.nps.gov/gewa
> 1732 Popes Creek Road, Colonial Beach
> 804-224-1732 (x227)
> Grounds open daily, 9am-5pm
> > Visitor Center open Wednesday-Sunday,
> > 9:30am-5pm, Memorial House open for tours
> > on the hour, 10am-4pm
> Entrance free

Trip 52 – Visit to Harpers Ferry with Hikes to Jefferson's Rock and the Maryland Heights

WHY: Harpers Ferry's history is a web of richly interwoven threads—the first military-industrial complex, the arrival of the first successful American railroad, John Brown's attack on slavery, the largest surrender of Federal troops in the Civil War, and one of the earliest integrated schools in the country. Or, you can just forget the history and enjoy the views of the confluence of the Potomac and Shenandoah Rivers where ducks and geese float nonchalantly down the rapids.

WHERE: From the Capital Beltway, go north on I-270 to Frederick and then take I-340 west toward Harpers Ferry. If coming from Virginia, take SR7 and then SR9 until just past Hillsboro where County Route 671 turns north toward Harpers Ferry. Turn left on I-340. From either direction, follow the signs on I-340 to Harpers Ferry National Historical Park Visitor Center. Take the free bus into Harpers Ferry (parking is limited there or nonexistent).

HOW LONG: The trip to Harpers Ferry takes about an hour. Allow a couple of hours for touring the town and the easy climb to Jefferson's Rock. After lunch, the hike around Washington Heights, about three and a half miles, takes almost two hours because the climb is steep and rocky.

LUNCH BREAK: There are numerous sandwich shops in town, or you can bring goodies from home for a picnic on the trail.

HIGHLIGHTS: At **Harpers Ferry National Historical Park**, start your visit at the Visitor Center, where you can pick up trail maps and information on park sights and activities before you board the bus for town. There is too much to see in one day—the town life exhibits, the Industry museum, and the John Brown, Civil War, Natural History, and African American History museums—a veritable cornucopia of history. Just to name a few famous names who helped shape Harpers Ferry history—Thomas Jefferson, George Washington, Meriwether Lewis, John Brown, Robert E. Lee, George Armstrong Custer and Frederick Douglas. Sometimes it's a surprise how they happened by.

Residents of the Washington area are likely to have visited here before so you might want to concentrate on the beautiful panoramas seen only by two climbs, one easy and one challenging. The first grand view is from **Jefferson's Rock**—a very short hike uphill from the town and well-marked. Jefferson described the view as "stupendous" and "worth a voyage across the Atlantic." The second panorama is reached across the railroad bridge, left along the C&O canal, and across the road to the **Maryland Heights Trail**. Take the green-blazed signs and then the red ones along the Overlook Cliff Trail to catch stunning views of Harpers Ferry and the confluence of the rivers. Hopefully a train will pass by far below as you gaze at the view. From the railroad bridge to the Overlook Cliffs is a 4.1 mile round-trip hike. You can go even further to the Stone Fort (blue- blazed Stone Fort Trail) where it straddles the crest of Maryland Heights at 1,448 feet. From the railroad bridge to the Stone Fort is six miles round-trip, which takes about four hours.

MORE INFORMATION

Harpers Ferry National Historical Park
www.nps.gov/hafe
Interactive map of Lower Town on website
171 Shoreline Drive, Harpers Ferry
304-535-6029
Open daily, 9am-5pm
Trails open sunrise-sunset
Entrance fee $20/vehicle; annual entrance fee $35

INDEX
(restaurants in bold)

A

B

D

E

F

G

O

P

Q

R

Made in the USA
Middletown, DE
19 December 2023

46361977R00109